E-RACE WHITE

Karen Kellock Ph.D.

E-RACE WHITE

PREFACE

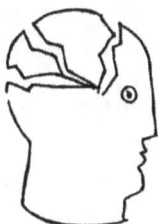

DIVERSITY IS _NOT_ OUR STRENGTH

We haven't lost our homeland tho' we live in dread and fear.   Mass immigration is underhandedly clever: the left found a way to attain power and hold it forever. Correct think: whites are oppressors and everyone else their victims for sure. America is a battlefield thru demographic change and population replacement. Even white people want the white race erased. But suddenly there's a wake up to the tragedy before us: being reduced to a hated minority in our own country which ancestors built and gave us. Women see how they've been misled and choose decency and family instead. The youth see the ridiculousness of college notions, how it's destroying our great nation.

WHITE

THE COMMUNIST SPIRIT (TAUGHT TO SHARE)

People take advantage of a good heart and it's heartbreaking to let em go but you must for a new start.

Communist spirit: "You have three, I have none so give me one".

When you encounter the communist spirit run the other way or quickly put up your boundaries.

Covetousness--acquisitiveness--is a common emotion so stop giving away your possessions.

The ability to say NO without feeling selfish is about boundaries so start practicing with this.

People have to respect you but also your things. It's not theirs but the communist spirit rings.

So you get nice things, can you keep em? A fool is easily separated from money or possessions.

MASS ILLEGAL IMMIGRATION

Diversity is not our strength, they're at each other's throats. It's just a utopian vision of Babylon.

Not wanting your people replaced is normal, natural and healthy.

Roman Empire was taken down by refugees.

Hijrah means demographic invasion.

The Kalergi Plan was to make everyone brown through mass illegal immigration and miscegenation.

WHITE

Through mass immigration the independent armed white man would minimize to nothing.

The non-whites are used to being disarmed, they'll vote for that not seeing the blatant harm.

In the world of multiculturalism and diversity, someone else's gain is always your loss, truly.

To make everyone brown is to make em controllable: the armed white man is their only obstacle.

Those who want diversity don't live in diverse neighborhoods, but are gated and protected.

See it as a pie: With each newcomer you are being displaced, your influence that much less.

We're being erased by being displaced but you can't see this not having empathy for your race.

928 machete attacks in London in just two months but mayor says it has nothing to do with migrants.

INVASION IS CALLED "ENRICHMENT"

Macron plans to enrich French society by importing 200 million Africans—it boggles the mind.

The Swedish feminist praises Islamic polygamy and ignores dark sides for the utopian reality.

Macron plans to enrich French society by importing 200 million Africans—feel grateful, Americans!

White ruling class with global homilists pushing a one world brown dystopia controlled by them.

The displacement of white Christians is a state-sanctioned dispossession.

Who's to blame is always "cuibono": who stands to gain.

WHITE

Much of the stuff happening to white people has been buried.

Evil Globalists: Put all the disparate groups together then take control and end all their independence.

Globalist eradication of differences: so they can no longer discern nor express their own interests.

They have no homeland but feel they own the world.

Taking down our cultures then flooding Europe with millions a year with radically different values.

Across the world populism and nationalism is blooming. We can win despite millions flooding in/fuming.

Humanity is coming out of its slumber/trance.

We're to be a homogeneous world of mind-controlled atheists.

STRIP US OF RELIGION

They seek to strip people of their religions, families and even sexual identities to make em zombies.

Those who do not block their borders will be lost. Viktor Orban

Millions are flooding in and millions more about to launch, this is historical and mass murderous.

Globalists flooding Europe with millions a year then weaponizing them against the freer.

Here's where we take a stand or we lose everything.

UK/Europe crisis: This is historic and mass murderous, millions of jihadis are flooding Europe.

Christians are gentle so who gets appeased? It's the old saying a squeaky wheel gets the grease.

WHITE

Trump can't get into London but if you're a jihadist they pave the streets with gold as apologists.

A "nice" Christian man turning to Hinduism? Happens rarely but when it does, total destruction.

It's the fallen new age churches that want everyone the same color so "racism" will be no more.

Actually God made us all unique, also the nations. He didn't want a bunch of blobs/freaks on rations.

Do other religions give true peace, when terror looms large from error?

Churches wanting us all brown are workers for the New World Order as God made us unique/clever.

IMPRISONED FOR WORDS

By saying "words are violence" they can throw you in jail for assault through your verbiage.

"Give me your tired..." is just a 100 year old poem by a socialist so please just shut up.

They're coming to take advantage of us because we are people who create wealth/they can't resist.

They're fleeing the hellish societies they created for themselves cuz they simply don't have it.

Wherever you see white people they're creating wealth and migrants want that for themselves.

They can't do it--create wealth--so they come here to get ours while putting us in a hell.

We don't want riffraff hanging around here.

Whites have built the most successful, easy and pleasant societies in the history of the world.

WHITE

It is not racism to say low IQ races are violent and rapacious, it's just a fact but you can't face this.

Democrats are now the party of foreign voters, many illegal. Tucker Carlson

Venezuelans dying of starvation as the communists pass a law saying you can't call it starvation.

Without parent approval kids now change their race not just their gender: mentally ill pretenders.

Carbon taxes are a cash grab, the latest liberal scam and fad.

Liberals hate western civilization and Christianity, it's key component/basis for our great nation.

There are some rich whites but most are poor as blacks so don't listen to the liberal flack.

THIRD WORLD WAYS

In sum, they want to maintain their crazy third world ways but with a great first world income.

As our influence dwindles in our own country we'll become a despised remnant seen as cruelty.

When liberals wakeup they flee the shit holes they create then escape to and ruin our red states.

Comanches tortured everyone they met so stop telling me about the sweet loving Indians, get it?

The only safe defection from North Korea is Christian missionaries cuz they're the good guys.

Proof we're at the end: Invasion by people not our friends to whom our own government lends.

They killed 80 million of their own people and you liberals align with the Chinese? Evil, evil.

WHITE

Go ahead and serve your evil globalist masters, you'll be the first to go when they take over.

Diversity is nothing but the lowest common denominator making us hate them, him and her.

No worry, judge lets you off for rape cuz you didn't learn to respect women in your Muslim faith.

6 Nobel prize winners unanimous the diversity experiment has failed so let's go no further into hell.

SOCIAL TIME BOMBS

600,000 migrants in Italy a social time bomb and finally they see it and jumped on the bandwagon.

It's obvious France and Germany are the boss.

The EU wants obedient satellites but Italians say "enough is enough".

A Europe shaped like Merkel/Macron has no future.

To get your life back be a euro-skeptic.

Anyone who denies the current Islamization of Europe is an accomplice. Fratelli d'Italia

Saudi Arabia is funding it all: mosques, cultural centers and universities in the west, Europe, Italy.

Italy: What a shame to have fought wars for centuries against Islam only to lose it due to inaction.

The E.U. can go f**k itself. Matteo Salvini

Forcing unwilling populations to accept those now living amongst them.

Any new gov has severe repercussions throughout Europe--like deporting a million just like that.

WHITE

A disunified angry increasingly intolerant populace coming to the end of their rope as an experiment.

Merkel madness will take a generation to clean up while she walks away and shrugs.

Expect the Swedenization of Ireland. It's time to object to globalization tactics, Irishmen.

Italy represents a massive shift to euroskepticism and the evil EU's end.

Brexit marked a massive change in politics cuz it's all about immigration, forever changed.

Youth voting for the EU--pee yuu

Brexit was the first domino and it's a tidal wave now.

MASS IMMIGRATION SURGE

Don't take em in but divert money to camps near conflict zones so they return to family/country.

They come to west to breed us out while living on benefits and spreading Jihad--do you see that?

It may be this invasion will harden the west/bring us back to the best and destroy liberalism no less.

She's devil incarnate, the most evil person who's ever lived in Germany destroying her own country.

Migrant crisis or Islamic insurgency nuisance?

When high IQ countries invade the west they get rich and don't blow things up.

Breakthrough: Relieved Europeans now want rapid action and know that a new Europe is possible.

Sanctuary state governors or city mayors are criminals and should be locked up now.

WHITE

Sanctuary states protect criminals not citizens and thus they are gangster organizations.

Putting the interests of immigrants over citizens--that's how whacked out the left has become.

Truth is no defense in Canada because it may spark outrage against the invaders and more trauma.

They didn't start that way, dumb. It's from intermarriage with first cousins marking the whole region.

Every time a first cousin marriage the IQ down 15 points so the multitudes are really outa joint.

If Merkel isn't stopped Germany will not be German within a generation.

MERKEL MADNESS

Arrest her: Merkel is responsible for destabilizating the whole continent for generations to come.

The West doesn't have to be Merkeled if it doesn't want to be--we can stop this crisis now, see?

Diversity is a curse on any society. It erodes trust and makes building social capital impossible.

Guilt implanted: Even white men willingly wanna give up land to minorities who hate em.

Globalism destroyed identity/made us feel empty. Now we're refilling with symbols from our history.

Much new age drug and alcohol abuse was an attempt to fill the void left by globalism, annoyed.

Anywhere there is multiculturalism there is great sadness by whites on how dogs are treated.

WHITE

The United Nations wants to reduce our population AS they flood us with other nations/religions.

Whites' anti-ingroup preference reflects in voting non-white to show you're not a racist blight.

Ireland is now the "emerald isle of Somalia"

Gender: It's NOT a spectrum but a bimodal distribution including effeminate men/mannish women.

If you say it's inborn (IQ, intelligence) that automatically makes you a racist in their eyes I guess.

CRIMINAL COMMUNISTS AT TOP

Communism: Rapists/murderers were put in charge since politics made them that way by and large.

Isn't it interesting how it's only white countries getting mass immigration from the third world?

Whites can't escape and white flight's declared as racism.

"Racism" is an anti-white hate slur.

"Diversity" just means less/no white people.

Immigration without assimilation is invasion.

In a low IQ society aggression is a strength and empathy a weakness so being peaceful fails.

With a cultural IQ of 80 and raised brutally will they ever be child-friendly? Not predictably.

Just be accepting of their harsh/crude ways. You don't wanna be unaccepting do you? Not ok

We are weak but reasonable and logical. They are strong and violent and die hard radicals.

WHITE

The threshold of what is acceptable has been lowered and it's a scare as we've become cowards.

The Epitome of Bull: Diversity is a strength but if you dare disagree with me I will destroy you.

Harboring criminals is the left's screwy view of citizenship and if you don't agree you're a bigot.

How we're different: West is influenced by the Reformation, Renaissance and the Enlightenment.

It's not left vs. right but left vs. west.

The biggest thing in our history is mass immigration into the west from third world countries.

Tens of millions are ready to embark in our direction.

MASS IMMIGRATION AND SUPERSTATES

Using mass migration to abolish the nation-state for a super-state is not new but makes us blue.

A nation is not just birth and origin but a tribe and groups of people vs. mass dejection/confusion.

Get off my case you stupid snitch—instead of "witch" it's now "racist" and you're put on a list.

Mass third world immigration increases dependence on the state while not voting to diminish it.

Dumb populations vote bigger government and higher taxes, the opposite to views of patriots.

A nation is a people of order: there's a way we do things and it works (makes us happier)

A population voluntarily replacing itself is unprecedented in human history and insane, clearly.

WHITE

Could you see Japan choosing to replace itself with another group? Of course not, they're not fools.

Fact: Willingly gave up your culture when ancestors paid with their blood to give it to you intact.

Just an idea: the left hates nations or anything but oneism--One Worldism--tho' it's a scam.

LOSS OF OUR RICH CULTURE

We have a rich history/culture and to give your children Mogadishu is the most evil thing to do.

When white countries are filled with non-whites it's genocide not diversity

Left demonizes nationalism because it blocks their agenda and that's the bottom line in America.

To describe the Germans as white people with a common ancestry is a hate crime now--WOW.

Blatantly telling Swedes that it's not their country anymore and to make room for New Swedes.

No place to go if opening our homes to the world and it becomes unlivable, I know cuz I was a fool.

It's young males all over the world invading, raping and destroying.

Think of it: the gangs, the invaders, all the trouble is from young males.

If not cool with this total and rapid transformation you're a racist cuz diversity is our strength.

Whites celebrate their own displacement and everyone but their own people and it's unbelievable.

You can't change demographics of a nation without a cultural, economic and political transformation.

WHITE

Israel to remain Jewish = cultural pride. White Christians want the same = horrible and denied.

They are seeing that socialism never works/goes against nature just as nationalism takes over.

People are tribal in nature--caring more for their own nation than a foreign nation, for sure.

PEOPLE ARE TRIBAL: FACT

People are tribal--that's a fact--and some BS fantasy or utopian ideology won't change that.

Just a matter of time until EU collapses but the question is: how much damage in the meantime?

East Europe just got their country back from failed socialism they're not about to hand it to Islam.

Feminized girlie men and masculine women linked with evil satanic globalism for this invasion.

Karma for baffoons: Keep your eyes on Europe, things are gonna be very interesting soon.

Tradition is not the worship of ashes but the preservation of fire. Gustav Mahler

The fed up Germans call Merkel "Mother Terrorisa" or "people's traitor" shouting "lock her up".

Cold to begs and tears, Germany will take in more than a million new refugees next year.

Merkel keeps testing the limits of Germany's political consensus.

Our freedom they see as blasphemy, our logic is their hatred, our free speech they detest, furious.

Blasphemy laws only pertain to offending Islam, never Christian.

WHITE

Price for multiculturalism: offending and being offended but blasphemy laws are only for them.

Blasphemy Laws are not to protect religion, but only Islam.

Blasphemy laws are Sharia creep.

Food line: Young male migrant pushes aside an elderly lady so German state calls her a "Nazi".

The liberals would call us bringing in white African farmers facing genocide "racist", you can bet on it.

When the liberals rule: recycled water from sewers ok'd for California taps-- wow how cool.

MURDER OF WHITES IS HIGHER

The murder of whites in South Africa is twelve thousand percent higher than blacks in America.

The major race science claim: there is more difference between groups than within them.

It's the biggest genocide in human history, the final solution to the white Christian European problem.

You can only get into the UK if an extremist, non-extremists are 86ed.
Muslims vote left in the west.

Go Trump, our most wonderful president, without whom the witch Hillary woulda let them all in.

Climate change is nothing but a man-made lie. It's just globalism arresting those who defy.

Stone age or primitive people in an unspoiled landscape isn't automatically pure, pristine they ain't.

In primitive societies the more they killed the more wives and children they had: the status of cads.

WHITE

In current academia, conformity to orthodoxy takes precedence over scientific methods.

Pseudo science of "radical racial egalitarianism" is false but you're good if you adhere and evil if not.

Tho' totally false, lives are destroyed if they don't agree to perfect egalitarianism, truth betrayed.

Races' different diseases: whites have terminal cuckishness or pathological altruism for sleazes.

Atheists are radical anti-science fundamentalists and zealots.

ATHEISTS BETRAY SCIENCE

Atheists have betrayed science, undone religion and opened up the west to this terrible mess.

Societies that treat women the best are dying off, those who treat them the worst are flourishing.

It's economics that makes them bad so if we give em a house, car and cash they'll be nice instead. Not

Violence is from lack of resources? Most terrorists are middle class so how does this argument exist?

If the benefits dry up the migrants go back.

If you can't see a barbarian when it's blatantly right in front of you that means you're one too.

Women don't have children so they wanna mother the migrants. Stefan Molyneux

The better the climate the worst the government, it's a tradeoff.

If the Black Lives Matter ever got the power here, that is the government of South Africa.

WHITE

We don't hear about white African slaughter so we see into the future like white minorities oughta.

They don't want us to see what happens with whites a minority in an aggressive, tribalized world.

We all know where it goes with anti-white hatred instilled: in a tribalized society they'll all be killed.

Appeasement is the hope the crocodile will eat you last but it's coming and it's hungry. Stefan Molyneux

UNSTOPPABLE ANTI-WHITE SNOWBALL

African chances of stopping the anti-white snowball exploding diminishes daily and it's frightening.

If we don't learn the lessons from white South Africa it'll come here and we'll be the minority, betcha.

Is it true that white liberal feminists are maternal to dogs and migrants but hate their husbands?

When that demographic change occurs everything will be gone for us while they flood/surge.

The Omnibus Spending Bill builds walls for Lebanon, Egypt and Jordan but nothing for us, man.

Diversity plus proximity equals war.

Blacks and Hispanics have been begging for the wall cuz it undercuts their wages and no one cares.

Europe's current leaders and the pope don't react to this invasion as they did in the middle ages.

The term "progressive" sounds so sophisticated--that's why they like it--but it's just pinheaded.

WHITE

The desire of whites surviving as a distinct people is being swallowed up by fear of being seen as evil.

What a predicament for whites and y'all: Having to make a moral case for your own survival.

Whites sympathize with cultures who's existence is threatened but not their own--what an enigma.

Whites very sad when the last speaker of obscure language dies but not about their own kind.

Every nonwhite country has the right to preserve its culture, but not white America that's for sure.

WHITES NEED THEIR SEGREGATION

Segregation not integration is how they keep obscure dying species alive, but not for us whites.

Why are whites the only ones explaining why they have a right to survive? Diversity is white genocide

Of two races creating delightful charming places to live (Asian or American) why do *we* have to give?

Japan is for Japanese only, though many from the third world would like to come in and enjoy it.

Migrants don't see generosity when they see Europeans (do they ever say thank you?) just weakness.

No backbone to maintain what's theirs, nor the morality to keep birthright safely for their heirs.

We could be disarmed and destroyed due to our virtues, foolishly lavishing on alien users.

They have no desire to be like us but easily take everything we have and we just adjust, even gush.

WHITE

Others have a right to have what we have and we do not have a right to keep it, what a gimmick.

Suicidal double standard where all groups can press for their bids but whites aren't permitted to.

Since they cannot explain racial differences they always say the disparity is from white wickedness.

It's the same double standard in Sweden: whites always to blame and the others all the rave.

The most curious phenomena is the number of whites who have swallowed this self-loathing.

Every nation considers itself superior to it's neighbors and every nation is right. French Proverb

Good Christian nations let em all in. Suicidal interpretation of the bible.

Fooled to hell thinking it's a wonderful blessing to be displaced by people unlike ourselves.

Why he won: He promised to send home every illegal immigrant, build a wall, possible Muslim ban.

A race realist and white advocate not "white nationalist" but we deserve our own place as majority.

Merkel, Hitler--whats the difference except the former is subtler but it's still invasion/murder.

LOW IQ IS VIOLENCE, HIGH IQ IS REFINEMENT

The people who tell us how wonderful diversity is can escape it--aren't we sick of these hypocrites?

It's a derangement exclusive to only one group: Whites giving away what is theirs, the whole scoop.

WHITE

When you get disparate groups into society it's no longer about ideas but theft and defense.

It's important that the left wants to import low IQ voters--wonder why they need the losers.

Hispanic immigration is the death of the republican party, small government and free market.

The rules are changing with immigration cuz they want big government and so what if we don't?

The more immigrants the more Obamavotes.

If you want small government focus on immigration as the more come in the more socialist/corrupt.

The problem isn't so much Hillary corruption it's that the democrats don't care/no compunction.

DIVERSITY IS THE DEMCRAT BASE

Democrats can say "diversity is our strength" because for them it's true--it's their voting base.

The facts are clear: the higher your ethnic diversity the higher your violent crime, vs. peaceful whites.

To get votes the left is willing to have people raped, assaulted, murdered, kidnapped, forsaken.

Left are power junkies living in gated communities unconcerned with devastation from policies.

They don't care who suffers with them getting more political power, the object of their addiction.

As government gets bigger as desired by invaders it continues to increase till you're 3rd world/deceased.

All over America, neighborhoods changed forever with no public debate.

WHITE

For the people who live there, it's traumatic.   Diversity for thee, but not for me.

Anarcho-Tyranny: Refuse to control criminals (anarchy) so come down on the innocent (tyranny).

They just don't live like us and they say the same too, so what?

So many slaughtered disproving myth that: we're all the same.

The worst punishment: to be thrown in with all of em.

In the UK the Muslim rapists are always labeled "local residents", "Asians" or "Oxford men."

America: Do not fall as we have fallen, do not become the UK, fight for your freedoms every day. Katie Hopkins

Whites ostracized as others have ethnic identity/strong in-group preference but we aren't allowed to.

Elites don't suffer from mass migration/multiculturalism--they reap the rewards, we pay the price.

Young male migrants pushing ahead of an elderly lady and the Germans react by calling her a "Nazi".

They say since we benefit the most from it, we are unaware of it--white privilege = their narrative.

EVIL EFFECTS OF DIVERSITY

Elites don't suffer from mass migration/multiculturalism--they reap the rewards, we pay the price.

Whites ostracized as others have ethnic identity/strong in-group preference but we aren't allowed to.

Young male migrants pushing ahead of an elderly lady and the Germans react by calling her a "Nazi".

WHITE

The left calls anyone for immigration restrictions as a "right wing hick" or a "backwoods nativist".

As mass immigration increases diversity it reduces social cohesion and civic trust: stop it or bust.

California's skid row is now a vast sea of broken people, rats and human waste. Katie Hopkins

They say since we benefit the most from it, we are unaware of it--white privilege, their narrative.

THREE NEUROSES OF THE LEFT

Three neuroses of the left: cognitive dissonance, narcissistic rage and psychological projection.

"Foreigners shall not in any way partake in the political matters of the country". Mexican constitution

Appeasement: The more we're threatened by em the more we pander to em.

We're supposed to let the whole world in then fight over scraps of our economy in a trash bin.

America is a battlefield and the battle is thru demographic change and population replacement.

"Foreigners shall not in any way partake in the political matters of the country". Mexican constitution

California's skid row is now a vast sea of broken people, rats and human waste. Katie Hopkins

Appeasement: The more we're threatened by em the more we pander to em.

Obnoxious liberal overreach on guns gives us a shot in November--I told you Trump was clever.

Anti-Trump prosperity and freedom haters would actually join forces with pure evil to dump Trump.

WHITE

Our great president has a fifty percent approval and with his reaction to the caravan it's quickly rising.

That's our man, we must rely on him--don't let em in cuz the caravan would just be the beginning!

Invading army is approaching--did they hear about the massive spending bill? This is pivotal.

Skills-based hiring is now racist.

Most of the people who voted for Trump aren't at war, they're at work. Michael Savage

MODERN CHURCHES AND DENS OF DEVILS

They aren't churches they're dens of devils. Alex Jones

All left is radical by nature, wanting to destroy the social order.

Racism of the worst kind is saying you can only be racist if white.

Trump: Act now congress, our country is being stolen.

America is the problem, not the virtuous ones breaking in. We impede their progress so shut up/obey.

We're to blame for everything so let the virtuous ones in and they'll redeem us.

The new immigration is an army of people who don't bother with paperwork.

Hand the left a victory and they just move on to the next thing.

Tearing down statues is so sad as I'm living in a hyper-present tense with no connection to my past.

Trump has full authority to repel attack on the border. Ann Coulter

"We're rich, they're poor and oppressed--let them in!"

Trump has full authority to repel attack on the border. Ann Coulter

WHITE

The caravan invasion is a test and an opportunity to see if Trump will react with {promised} integrity.

That crazy 2018 generation said there were infinite sexes and you could be any race you wanted.

U.N. plan: Once they bust open a hole they'd invade, flood and take over the country as a whole.

DACA = democrat voters, power, lotsa money.

Oversaturated in leftist BS that everyone can come here, the caravan event cues wall (get-er-done)!

The reason women are lousy voters is the appeal to emotion and everyone knows that's a bad decision.

Women are lousy voters because they go for abortions, wear pussy hats and want open borders.

STATISTICS: WOMEN VOTE LEFT

It's a matter of statistics what women vote for so don't take offense but it's something to abhor.

"Helping to save the world/charitable" when actually they're ruining the country/it's irrevocable.

Democrats have ruined every city they rule.

It's all about appearances with the left: to look like they're helping rather than actually helping.

Looking past their facade you can see democrats have no substance.

Trump using cashcow NAFTA to punish Mexico for being so incompetent and criminally dangerous!

SJW's don't care about genocide in S. Africa cuz they're white.

WHITE

When liberals say they're pro-immigration they mean non-white, non-Christian immigration.

The globalist liberals want immigrants from Muslim or socialist Latin American countries.

What they want is a disarmed, dehumanized and infantilized populace who is easily controlled.

LIBERALS WANT MEDIA DOMINATION

The liberals want full global/media domination--they're globalists--and could care less about US.

Caravan pushed Trump for a stern and speedy response--Dems always do themselves in like this!

The caravan did us a favor: raising the issue to be seen as extreme and outrageous, it's a changer.

It's time for Daca to end/the wall to rise up, along with the American people who are sick of this evil.

Socialism is really creepy as people start eyeing your things. It makes one feel guilty/lives changed.

ISIS and Al Qaeda come into the US through Honduras along with Syrians so it's not just Mexicans.

The president is a dictator when it comes to the border and non-citizens.

It's a classic globalist attack to break up our sovereignty--we're five years behind Europe today

Trump has massive power at the border since it's the executive branch's main purview.

Canada is sinking cuz Trudeau was raised by a crazy feminist mom and distant dad: single mom kid.

WHITE

This demographic stealth invasion is much more permanent and dangerous than a Normandy-style one.

Theresa Mae: open borders advocate, phony feminist, virtue signaler, traitor to race/culture.

Why gun control? Because armed people won't get into boxcars voluntarily. History Lesson

THE SUCKING SPIRIT

Be cautious of the sucking spirit that wants to take things from you so that it can be theirs.

Communist spirit: if you have three and I have one you *owe* me one: liberals are terrible/no fun.

The successful, intelligent, informed mavericks and trailblazers all know this new authoritarianism.

Leech defined: Sticky fingers, sucking spirit.

When one gives you something never ask for more or you'll never see em again if they're mature.

Give gifts to an evil person and he just wants more and this is his karma: you shut the door.

Giving to them gives em the idea to hit you up for more--it was the trigger for all you abhor.

Giving acts as a trigger as they ask for more cuz it's a new idea they never thought of before.

If you give em something and they ask for more they've poor character and you know it for sure.

WHOLE GENERATION OF THIEVES

I thought it was isolated incidents of theft but it's a whole generation with spirt of communists.

WHITE

It doesn't matter that it was just a pencil it's still not theirs and respect for private property is rare.

You're never allowed to store in quantity, the liberals want it and they deserve it is their fantasy.

Just cuz they demand it doesn't mean you have to give it. People eye your things and want it.

With the house a leaky boat cuz you lend to a toad it's like a sucking spirit/you're outa control.

They saw it and they want it, period. That's the child in adults and we're darn sick of it.

Le Femme and the Communist Spirit: my next book about this school-bred mentality: fear it.

When that sucking spirit wants what you own that's when your house becomes a leaky boat.

If your friends are the borrowers your house is like a leaking boat and hey man, you're outa control.

Don't let people take things from your house. Show them where to get it on their own, the louse.

When people ask to borrow do you feel uncomfortable? Do you give in to be "nice" to the rabble?

Everything you bought was cuz you wanted it. Stop lending it cuz that's the last you'll see of it.

Those things are there because you wanted them, where do they get off upsetting your plans?

YOU'RE NOT SELFISH

It has nothing to do with you being "selfish" so get offa that thing--they just saw you coming.

WHITE

She's not your friend but your foe--because of her your house is unsecured/a leaky boat.

She took advantage and I'm a dam pushover. A recluse doesn't know any better but it's still a fetter.

Sucking spirit grabs on then bleeds you.

The guts of globalism is about being heartless, soulless, and using other people, seen as "strength".

Since everyone wants a piece of me I gotta have him betwixt me and thee.

Leech, sucking spirit = leaky boat/fear it.

1400 years this religion has created giant armies of inbred insane people resulting in deformities/evil.

Sucking spirit: grab on, bleed out.

When someone gives you something never ask for more lest you lose them & your future for sure.

Giving to them is the trigger to ask for more then they're out the door and what a relief--you soar.

You give, they want more. Another way of saying: give em an inch and they take a mile, clear?

Total domestication phase: half the country's on the dole.

People filled with the devil due to sin make mistakes, overreach and bring themselves down.

DEMISE OF THE LEFT

Diversity is a shakedown: shut up white people and pay up.

Grow government, get rid of middle class, transfer money offshore, make us dependent and poor.

WHITE

You got rid of God but now you've got the state which is much worse than God. Stefan Molyneux

In general, virtue increases as intelligence increases--then there's the bell curve of the vicious.

The New Right is about loyalty to one's own people (white Europeans) tho' that's all seen as evil.

Welfare is merely the method of transforming the market economy step by step into socialism.

It is difficult to free fools from the chains they revere. Voltaire

If you control the person's healthcare you control the person. Lenin

If socialists understood economics, they wouldn't be socialists. Frederick Von Hayek

Real Indians want local politics, fake Indians (Liz Warren) want centralized gov/a communist.

Demise of the left is the demise of global politics: a one-world cosmology and we're sick of it.

Migrants and leftists flock to the cities and I'm glad of that--stay away from the country, please!

Is it true the less we have in common the stronger we are?

No socialism in America as the poor feel like temporarily embarrassed millionaires. John Steinbeck

WOMEN ARE THE PROBLEM: MAD AT DAD

I'm a social psychologist so cultural mental illness is my business.

I'm mad at women for their virtue signaling calling it politics and their loving big gov/open borders.

WHITE

Children love having mother and father together. It's paradise on earth, birds of feather.

Hedonism came along and said to hell with it all just enjoy thyself: societal decay/family collapse.

Sex Ed is nothing but hardcore porn, a national disgrace as they impose this crap on five year olds.

Evil means to destroy the man by telling women he's vermin and paying them to leave em.

All men are horrible so if you say you're a victim you're in the cool club.

The laws must be changed: no more false accusations of child molestation in courts for leverage.

Educating the mind without educating the heart is no education at all. Aristotle

The old hippie called "Cher", the aging pop star, popped off about Trump calling him a cancer.

Enlightenment is not getting happier but the crumbling away of untruth--seeing through pretense.

Obama-led drone strikes killed innocent 90% of the time but she still loves this communist slime.

The people who don't know anything will never say "no" to anything. Mark Passio

I will call you "hate speech" if I hate the fact I can't argue back.

DOMESTICATE US TO KILL US

Domesticate us so we can't defend or feed ourselves, so they take control when it all goes to hell.

They didn't have fathers so were accosted/gave into young boys and it's been that way since.

WHITE

Without fathers they're always in withdrawal, symptoms: yelling, pleading, threatening, crying.

When you swim in muddy waters get a little mud on you and most from blue states have a little P-U.

Women are excited by men who are skeptical of their value. Stefan Molyneux

Obama/Hillary are literal demons (smell bad) but the selfish don't care, can you imagine that?

Doctrines of demons, sanctuary of devils: It's happening folks, the false church slippery slope.

Thank God sexuality is diminishing for me, it's like casting out a demon. – Socrates in his 70's.

Education is the kindling of a flame, not the filling of a vessel. Socrates

LIBERALISM THE DEFAULT SETTING

The brain is an organ damaged by education.

If you hate Trump you can do whatever you want and be totally forgiven/part of the club.

University liberals are given everything because they signed onto the globalist program/fiends.

We're in the grip of a fascistic leftist theocracy stifling, squelching, attacking anti-dogmatists.

Civilization ceases to exist when debate and reason is no longer allowed. Stefan Molyneux

Our commitment to free speech means the left must impose itself thru aggression, ostracism, rejection.

Without facts on their side they all become verbal abusers: slander is the tool of losers. Socrates

WHITE

Government is the great fiction thru which everyone seeks to live at the expense of everyone else.

Politicians and diapers must be changed often and for the same reason. Mark Twain

Donald loves Kanye West so how could he be a racist?

Trump has dragon energy: creative, disruptive energy. Shaking things up, golden age of vitality.

Kanye West should reject all who rejected him for loving Trump. Bet they're all women, huh.

Two ways to be fooled: believe what is not true or refuse to believe what is true. Soren Kierkegaard

Even tho' they were weak/mind controlled we have still turned us against them, tho' forgiven.

The hottest love has the coldest end. Socrates

Women aren't smart enough to process information running counter to emotional preferences?

I do so love Donald Trump. Kanye West

NRA raking in millions as a backlash against vermin so go ahead and protest more is comin'.

Just cuz you got em to go along with you doesn't make it right, good, intelligent or out of sight.

You can make people do what you want, I'll grant you that. It's a real talent but you're still a brat.

LIBERALISM EVEN IN CHRISTIANS

Christians going left in the American schism: letting in refugees and battling nonexistent racism.

WHITE

In healthy times, great nations are conscious of their past and anxious to pass on what has been won.

Self-hatred is implanted in your kids by vicious crybaby ideologues, a toxic environment.

In the world of secular liberalism you can abort your kids, you just can't spank em.

Stop letting mental pipsqueaks tell you what to think.

Secular Modernity is the globalist's cramdown and it's incomprehensibly evil, dirty and wrong.

Statistically women vote for open borders and bigger government so *they* are the problem!

Because they lead with their heart (a good start) they can't see the bigger picture/not real smart.

Caring about the welfare of animals is not a leftist but a humanist position.

Rosanne: All about economics not about 2016 cultural revolution—she missed that we're all sick of this.

Saying it's about economics is downplaying the immorality and sick invasion of feminism in politics.

Roseanne reflected Hollywood cramdown saying you "can't raise kids in traditional gender roles".

Trump is a cultural warrior elected due to blowback from gender role confusion/return to facts.

New Normal: Era of the Political Right.

GENDERS IN ALL CULTURES

Blowback: unintended consequences of brainwash. Cramdown: media inculcation by ideologues.

WHITE

It is not healthy to avoid reinforcing gender roles or to produce gender confusion in children.

Every single culture through time has gender-based dress, so boys become men to defend us.

The liberals contradict saying "clothes don't make a difference" so why put our boys in a dress?

The bible is very strict against cross dressing.

Shift from secular, modernist, transcultural liberal human rights paradigm to reality: yours and mine.

Civic nationalism: Whether black or white we were proud citizens of a country achieving so much.

Americana is a culture and strong tradition held together by common religious commitments.

Donald Trump ratings are up at 51% despite overwhelmingly negative (95%) media coverage.

How I know all: I had to learn to deal with juvenile pre-prison criminals to learn about liberals.

I didn't have to go to prison to learn it I got a big dose of invading liberal thieves in Borrego Springs.

INVASIONS OF LOVING LIBERALS

Loving liberals invaded me, brought all their friends to steal from me then evaded all responsibility.

See your foes as the scum bags they really are to return to the pleasure of knowing you're right, a star.

Pornography: broken families, loose relationships, malleable minds and shattered societies.

WHITE

Pornography shrinks frontal part of the brain (will power/moral compass) so he can't refrain.

Millennials don't wanna be with a human being cuz it's a 7 when a 10 {porn} releases dopamine.

Warning: People are loyal only in times of stability but weakness is attacked so keep your head up, ok?

Even 9 month old babies prefer toys specific to their gender. Biologically boys are defenders.

Even male monkey babies wanna play with trucks not dolls, ok?

Denialism--denying facts due to idealism--is such a huge study you can even get a Ph.D. in it.

Liberals think that if we don't end up the same, injustice is happening and the whites are to blame.

BE CAREFUL FOR WHITE BOYS

If you have a white boy be mindful of his school. Things have changed beyond recognition, uncool.

The feminist teachers indoctrinate through hysteria and it's the most serious thing in America.

If a child is told he is bad for his race it's so destructive it'll take years to undo, yet you say it.

I hate liberalism and wish we could have worthy debates but why do they always have to escape?

You want him to be all he can be so stop nagging at he.

One-ist cosmology: so inveterate, obdurate and completely laid out they think it makes em free.

Debauchery, ceaseless orgy is human history.

WHITE

Obama killed the economy then started race wars: total abuse of power yet libs love him more.

THEY WANT US FACELESS BLOBS

They want us without identity, to be malleable. Not a race, nation, religion, not even a gender.

If you don't have an identity it's very easy for cultural Marxists to give you one and it's nasty.

They overplayed it when we went from accepting queers to men in the bathroom marked "hers".

Every animal has self-defense and Jesus said if your enemy has a sword, get a better one fast.

Make yourself sheep and the wolves will eat you. Mark Twain

Equality of opportunity is freedom, equality of outcome is tyranny.

University: Blacks are never guilty of racism/whites are always guilty of racism, it's unconscious.

Machiavelli: How the haves keep power. Saul Alinsky: How the have-nots can take it away.

Mr. or Mrs. Superior give you sermons on how to conform to them and it's always virtue signaling.

He tortured us for eight years ending with the whole world hating us and it's *him* you miss?

College professor means: dumbness, abuse of power and mediocrity.

Why are women so stupid/shallow? They weren't born that way, just want each other's approval.

MEN SUPPORT WOMEN AND CHILDREN

WHITE

Men don't support the world for other men or "patriarchy" but for women and children, you and me.

Say the truth and offend everyone big time or stay quiet and warp your soul: think on this/decide.

Biggest myth: If we outlaw guns they won't be plentiful. But with prohibition they drank to their fill.

Feminists lie about campus rape culture, gender pay gap and the patriarchy-- it's all malarkey.

The 2nd amendment is for defense against criminal gov (rare) but mostly lunatic mobs creating terror.

We live in a republic which prevents the MOB from taking over our individual rights or love of God.

We need guns to protect against lunatic mobs for the left is most virulent and objection's not allowed.

Their idea of Christianity is virtue signaling on trendy topics, the ones most people agree with.

Whenever someone says "We're all God" or "all churches are the same" escape to where you came.

Their false religion compels them to push the envelope downstream until their total destruction.

Leftists dismiss religion as mental illness.

FREEDOM UNTIL FEMINISM

Other religions treat women like vermin but Christian men treat em like gold until wrecked by feminism.

Women were always rewarded the kids but now (with decay) judge gives em to a homosexual to raise.

WHITE

Our women enjoyed great liberty/freedom until feminism destroyed those privileges, long gone.

Men used to break their neck to open a door for a lady, now that's all gone due to feminism: shady.

"Male and female created He them" and that division is clear all thru scripture but not in Babylon.

Couple decades back they woulda bashed the male trash going into women's bathroom like that.

America's real men never tolerated this crap back then. How we long for those days back again!

And the same be said for some of you but now you're washed and changed as filthy sin's gone too.

The Bible makes every society happier and better so the devilish elites want it banned forever.

Why don't most churches ever talk about sin? Having no power they ignore it/throw in trash bin.

Our children are raised up right then slowly turn away as they're sucked into lies/deception every day.

Nothing has any meaning except as it relates to Him, and that's how a Christian is a Christian.

YouTube employees could be shot by someone banned by them as they're in a gun free zone.

Trump was elected against Hollywood cramdown of things like gender roles which Roseanne reflects too.

A POST-CHRISTIAN SOCIETY

In public and even church life, traditional morality grounded in Christianity has been discarded.

WHITE

You brought all your friends to our house and didn't think about our loss of privacy one bit--twit!

Let the far right be the new consensus, the new normal.

"Far right" was a pejorative term but now we're not just a margin we're the mainstream, growin'.

Threat to localized identity markers = reversion to national symbols to resist global invaders.

The new conservative age is literally transforming the entire world.

Never taught how to act they were brought up in a jungle in fact so I say stay away/never go back.

There is nothing more intolerant than secular liberalism.

The resurgence of nationalism entails a process of re-traditionalization.

Religion's common enemies are secular liberalism and jihadist terrorism.

Anti-social behavior is a trait of intelligence in a world full of conformists. Nikola Tesla

UK youth perturbed with older generations for voting Brexit--that's how outa touch and globalist.

If pedophelic all it takes is one glance/nod and that's it. Nothing discussed it's like an animal lit.

TIRED OF ARGUING WITH TEENS

Never argue with teens, support them in craziness cuz it will bring our win and they'll deflate.

Liberals: fat-acceptance is hitched to thin privilege.

They only want to return to their virtue-signaling and slamming of non-liberal realists.

WHITE

Why is he not working--is he looking at pornography? Cuz that stunts their growth completely.

It's a battle of narratives. If it's done by social utilities we're on a fast track to hell for you and me.

Ideology linked to color: Non-whites wanna take the guns and constitution doesn't matter.

Help him to be all he can be not by scolding and yelling but leading, encouraging, being.

No I don't wanna go to your picnic and be attacked by flies. I wanna stay home and be amazed!

FRIEND

If you're a thinker or tinkerer, you gotta manage people. You have hours, protectors, locked doors.

Loyalty to the group must transcend autonomy but I couldn't do that you see: I wanted my liberty.

That I'd rather stay home alone than go to a social was just too much to those without goals.

Every time I went out I wished I'd stayed home. I just never left paradise again, never to roam.

Nothing out there can compare with life in here. If only women knew this life would seem fair.

Success is not from east or west but from God who puts one down as he makes the other renowned.

Prepare to come out of obscurity. I know it's like a blanket of cozy security, being holed in constantly.

Social is the whole thing--as it degrades so too their corny personalities and true genius is a rarity.

I will never be in that rejecting matrix again. I'm out of it and don't care if you're my friend.

They think they are so funny but entirely corny cuz they cheer each other on in their own reality.

FRIEND

If you're alone God has singled you out for a job and doesn't want other influences messing it up.

I wanna stay home with the wind and my pets. Not smile and laugh, answer questions/deal with pests.

I went thru terrible things to learn the lesson: build a high wall or this day you won't be enjoyin'

Husband loves it too: High walls, locked gate. He says in amazement: "I never felt this way!"

Life has shocks and betrayals when it all goes upside down. In an instant we go humble from renowned.

You have enemies? Good--that means you stood up for something. Winston Churchhill

In the end we will remember not the words of our enemies but the silence of our friends. M.L. King

Think of their insult. Don't drink or eat it down, face it. Now overcome the crazy nuts and make it.

Now's the time to think ahead: success--outa old systems keeping you down/creating a mess.

There were no lost years as underneath something was brewing that went way beyond tears.

Payback is your success. God promised it after you planted the seed to transcend this mess.

Payback is something you gotta see--you never did one darn thing for me and now we're family?

FRIEND

He acts so nice then tosses you a zinger, one that takes forever to get over.

I couldn't understand those who knew everyone's name and number while I lived in an ivory tower.

I felt invaded by everyone, it seemed I never had time alone. They'd get angry cuz time was my own.

The new age hates those with convictions and goals cuz it makes them feel less, that's taboo.

You fear going out there tho' that is your role. Give this to God, He'll see you through/console.

Just work in the morning then spend all day getting ready for the next morning, you'll be soaring.

Man, you were just my springboard to a higher life--my reward after going through so much strife!

The value of privacy is not realized until it is lost.

Regimen: Work from 3 - 8 am. Rest of the day get high (receptive) for next morning preparation.

These quips are whatcha call "essentially true".

Deceitful relationships bring gut aches constantly then other people hop on adding fuel to your misery.

Solar plexus is felt in gut--it tells you there's discordance in your environment, you're in a rut.

You're in denial but your solar plexus (GUT) isn't and it may explain your headaches too: listen.

FRIEND

Frenemies are usurpers and foes and it's even in your family, you know. It's this era/wish it weren't so.

Denial--a safety mechanism for survival?

To forgive, go back into denial and live.

If you are not rehorrified at the ridiculous you'll be resavaged in adapting to that environment worse.

The day and hour of world success cannot be predicted but can be anytime since the work is done.

Every sentence is saying the same thing in a different way.

I've done all I can, wrote a 1400 page book about how crazy they are. Now I'll retire/you do your part.

Don't pain for those who left you: use it for your success and going ahead-- don't you want that?

Think of their insult. Now use that to galvanize energy for improvement and total success, do it.

Befriend my foe, you're out the door.

Prejudice. Use the insult to galvanize energy for total success and never see them again.

You win and rule cuz you know how to do things best. Resisted all the way, finally you're the head.

Do your work/pray = way ahead of the game.

If you feel it speak it cuz you're speaking to us all--we went through it all too: LIFT US:

FRIEND

The dumber they are the more social! Think of that when they bug you to go but you don't want to.

I escaped the social mazeway of a small desert town by moving way out, then real lessons began.

I learned to love my cabin in the wilderness, my waterloo, my nemesis for what I'd been through.

Lessons were about boundaries and assertion: Don't come here, get out: that was my education.

I was invaded by thugs and police wouldn't protect me--that's just like now, it's a world tragedy.

If you've got liberal characteristics I'm gonna see it.

You should release with love but sometimes you first gotta release with hate, but do it anyway.

I'm thru feeling rejected by you so I release you now and that's like a big Christmas present too.

Build your fence before they make it illegal, like Houston. Can you believe that--they want us down.

Although there are brilliant thinkers like me most women are stark raving mad, they just can't see.

If you wanna be alone that's when they'll invade. They get a little restless and wanna make you pay.

Instead of raging with frustration at the interruption learn to see it as a lesson: need more assertion.

FRIEND

If you feel inspired, if God's given you an assignment, you must detach--that's your achievement.

It is not freeing or expanding to be social, it's more like a prison. Break out, be free, spirit is risen.

Separate/solitude = sanctified/holy.

It's especially hard for female genius since solitude is a hideous stigma in this generation I guess.

A captured soul collapses in Stockholm Syndrome then can't say "no" and is taken completely over.

Lack of assertion or boundaries means evil flows in and you're either dead or a life failure instead.

People can't do more than their genetically programmed to and if you correct they'll get mad too.

They can't see it, period. It's outa their frame of reference so open up to another or you'll be out of it.

You're asking for delicacy, tact, refinement--they don't have it and never will. It's genes, get real.

85% of communication is non-verbal so don't listen to words, read body language signs if you're able.

You're asking legless men to run a race. They just can't do it, they don't care and it's best to escape.

Repartee: Adroitness and cleverness in reply.

FRIEND

Fallen Hero Syndrome: everyone jumps on the bandwagon to bring him down, that's the human pound.

God said: Stop adding fuel to the fire and I'll erase this right now.

For there shall be no reward for the evil man; the lamp of the wicked shall be put out. Prov 24: 20

Do not associate with those who are given to change or allegiance. Prov. 24: 21.

Take away the wicked before the king, and his throne will be established in righteousness Prov 24: 25.

Your problem is trying to sell yourself rather than doing something great.

I'll never let you uglify my surroundings again.

A poet is an ocean of emotion so when things go wrong it's a Tsunami: watch out, much commotion.

Attitude is great but how can you have one if you don't know what the heck you're talkin' about?

Virtue signaling marks the liberal--that's how we know.

Shut up with your attitude thing, making a fool of yourself spouting off like you know everything.

Born clear, we mal-adapt to an insane world and become dense. Seen that way it all makes sense.

I just spoke the truth as I saw it at that moment. Can't even remember what it was, I just trust it.

FRIEND

Adults are a haunted house as early traumas determine perception and I'd hate to be their victim.

You can't have personality without knowledge to pull it off. Build your identity/style, know your stuff.

Things happen, who can explain em, just trust Him.

A series of severe shocks then she changed the locks and returned to her own reality which rocks.

You don't have to give into demands. Stand your ground against the spirit of the communists.

All the glory goes to God because it's Him coming thru but you'll get all the worldly credit and soon.

I went thru dark slums/scary people/had burdens in learning scruples but the reward's so cool.

The Creative Act is a literal structure in nature, with a beginning and an end. Like a diamond.

You will know when you're done, but Einstein said "you cannot ever know until that point it's done."

We built a home together and it began by escaping California.

Forgive yourself for the demons with whom you kept company.

Forgive, forget and never speak of it again. Because of Jesus it doesn't exist, He erased the sin.

If He came thru the Creative Act He'll also smooth it out. He'll send His angels so let out a shout!

FRIEND

You've worked all your life, you've overcome so much. Now you've arrived and are remunerated, a bunch.

Keep on envisioning, creating, solving, overcoming, building and your time will come if you faint not.

It's archetypal: pre-success crises.

Einstein just woke up in fame. He'd worked all his life but it seemed overnight his world had changed.

Your remorse over eras when you were controlled by the devil: It's erased along with all evil.

Stop making up your own religion.

I couldn't live in town, it had to be nature so what could I do but take an existing shack, a humbler.

Let the reward be appreciation for what you've already been given.

Ok, so you don't wanna work. I can understand that, bye.

So take a million selfies you narcissist--abusing modern science for your boring self-indulgence.

You've had it up to here! Now's the time for delicious life change way ahead by light years.

It's not stuff/temporary events! They're over/gone then you're depressed? It's eternity you nuts.

Nothing feels so good as enantiodromia: system inversions where those on bottom now rule ya.

FRIEND

Ignore looks, status, time spent. Superficials are the devil's devices unworthy of God's attention.

The great thinkers become philosophers or die in the gutter as rejected and scorned failures.

How can a thinker or poet adapt to that? Nothing makes any sense so they just get drugged up.

The greatest saints were the worst sinners cuz they learned most from their mistakes and the Savior.

As horrible as it was, God was with me and He didn't give me more than I could take, but it sure took.

Just one little thing: if you take the ball and run with it, eternity, blessings, no more stressing.

She didn't get it, as usual it's the wrong emphasis.

It's your fault and they're good. What else to think when they're all the same, but it's social hypnotism.

Now we need protection from others. Fortunately we love our neighbors and they love us.

It's too late for them and life is short. You gotta get on with it and then you can make your mark.

We tend to get attached—but it's turns sick. Put your focus back on God and everything is fixed.

It's always been this way, hon': God's men stuck on the periphery until their time has come.

FRIEND

Everyone looks down on the superior men but success is reward for overcoming the challenge.

Don't you want that: to show the creepy haters who said it couldn't be done and see them go splat?

The only thing is: if an individual lover of truth you'll be alone but will learn to love going SOLO.

GO SOLO. So long, so low: I thought you had it all but wrong, just another bore in the throng.

God's timing: It's a day, hour and minute. Before that split second you're an unknown, even hated.

You have a rare knack no one else has. Human genius has infinite variety cuz God loves just us.

Push those creepy snobs outa your head cuz they don't pay rent there and never saw you as rare.

They've caused you aggravation so now stop your premature aging as God restores youth again.

The devil's crowd will always hold you down and you're outa grace cuz it's not where you belong.

God's done so much, forget those who blocked/creeped you out--they're only human/focus on God.

Those getting huffy at correction will make big mistakes requiring exaction.

Now let's go back to your household: the real queen is never seen but subtly sets the scene.

Don't try to make them see for they will never see. Just see them then realign to stay free.

FRIEND

Just cuz they say they can do the job doesn't mean they can so trust your guts not what is said.

Don't try to explain why trust is lost, just get away. These are now your enemies and they're not ok.

She got huffy with correction then proceeded to make the same mistake again. Predictable, huh

Where truth is gone it's all an outward show. Being nice, saying the right things, being aglow.

Huffy over correction, made mistake again.

Can't yell at the incompetent, all you can do is see them then re-align to maintain your freedom.

Stop giving importance to people yet never thinking of God. This is false religion: people-worshippin'

It's scary as ego alien material arises from collective unconscious but Jesus saves us from this.

Stop. Ponder. Don't compulse, focus.

Suddenly, in the twinkling of an eye, you'll meet the link to all the connections you'll need.

Don't compulse, you'll meet him in an elevator or other coincidence so: relax after great diligence.

Who cares—put em all in a bag to go out. Look at all their pics, put em in a folder, delete, shout.

Stop explaining yourself, it's a sign of weakness. It's them who explain themselves to you, or else.

FRIEND

 Attachments (even through hate) are clouding your image which is destiny, fate, predesigned genius.

Cult of fame and red carpet lame. It's sickening to see your own kin display silly narcissist games.

The lowminded take 1000 pictures of themselves and it's death by a thousand cuts as wisdom falls.

For success, control your mind. No tangents or resentments and work things out before night.

Who cares what they think? They're insane or wouldn't have been attracted to you then, a fink.

Don't ever think of em, they're in the trash/recycle bin.

Forget em, they didn't want you. Think on that, let it make you great through and through.

I'm an isolate, don't like being seen but it's about the copy not me.

Hold back strength, don't work, listen to music/party as you wait for perks as leisure inspires works.

Breakups: They didn't want you--that's reason enough to never think of em again, now stop it.

They're just people, get over it. Love God He is preeminent.

They clearly thought no one was going to know/they could get away with it.

It doesn't matter what they think only what God thinks.

You can control him you just can't let him know.

FRIEND

Get some class. Take ONE picture of yourself, picking the best.

The social game: take pictures of yourself smiling like you're having the party of your life, beguiling.

Assemble a duffle of quintessential: most essential of all, to be ready to move when hearing the call.

Wipe that smirk off your face. Life is serious and you gotta ace. Focus, think of us, state your case.

The reason you should be serious/focused is trouble may come. No jocularity or running around.

Don't bemoan being alone cuz that's how you got so good and knowin'

Never let em frame you, frame yourself cuz true friends are few.

It is so dark, so frustrating--but likely part of the process: pre-success crisis.

Suddenly they see how empty they are. The ontologically fatal insight: it was all an illusion, bizarre.

Compromised Christians seek to be nice/not step on toes--weaklings unfit for the kingdom, foes.

Since they don't read the bible they think it's about social, hospitable, nice, with many friends.

Just cuz things aren't happening this minute, they panic. Learn patience: let it fall into a fabric.

You've had nothing but trouble so it's what you still expect-- but things will be easy now as God's Elect.

FRIEND

Only the smart can see the value. They're rare now so don't get down cuz everyone's so shallow.

You prayed, asked God to dissolve the block and got with brethren so now relax as it all fills in.

You must realize your potential while here on earth so don't waste a minute with framers/be alert.

Framers of your identity--either from past systems or ideology--will block your genius destiny.

There's no possible way for your joy with that going on in your home and I think you know that hon'

You can't be around that sort of thing even if it is your own kin. No boyfriends, locked doors, sin.

You had your chance backstabber it's called the big payback so go ahead with smiling and chatter.

This isn't the fifties, gone is all decency. But under my roof? No way missy

Parents afraid of putting their foot down, fear of insults all around? Now's the time to be strong!

Don't ever give up, where there's will there's a way, your faith is just being tested on this rainy day.

Things seem so bad you wanna end it all. Looks bleak but then prayer brings light/ends the stall.

The defining characteristic of anorexia is a wish to die. Jill Holm-Denoma

It is genetic and the symptoms roll out with stress as it does with all genetic illnesses.

FRIEND

Just wait for the link. God has it planned but waiting for that moment it may stink/you need a shrink.

Some women don't mind weight gain even big as a house, others may panic over a few pounds.

Man adapts to his environment like all animals. If it's sick and mixed up, it'd be a miracle to be on top.

What is maturity? It is unpeeling the cultural neurosis making us all crazy.

Sold me out, put me in chains. You had it all arranged, you handed me over, I felt so betrayed.

Took my money, got my honey, didn't want me to see what you're doing to me, payback not funny.

So let me get this: You're impressed with their outward success so can ignore the mess I guess?

Lives filled with correspondence, but is that all there is? No inner journey or sense of coincidence

In the old frontier, life was hard and often hideous. Danger being imminent, photos were serious.

The youth act like nothing can ever happen. Smiling, faking, the endless circus of corny distractions.

They are so woefully unprepared for hardship they'll drown in their toxins/fall by the wayside.

As political/economic freedom decreases, sexual freedom compensatingly increases. Aldous Huxley

FRIEND

 Shocking stats: 70% of Christian men view porn regularly and the rest just sometimes, Lord help me!

Jesus said it's in the eyes: Porn is a form of adultery, something to despise.

Not just porn but flirts with clerks--so many marriage-debasing and adulterous actions by jerks

Any pastor who says he's gotta view smut to get it up is a liar, phony and adulterer/leave, STOP.

Shocked and hurt lady said: "I hate all his crap around, I hate him. I want him gone and his sin".

Wait for Jesus to turn it all around. He knows what's happening and will vindicate His own.

Shock, what to do: Reach out to friends and those who don't reply, END. Music/goin' on ahead.

Ontologically fatal insight: the world is not what you thought--your world has flip-flopped.

Now look ahead: far better than what you've had, a life of dread.

Champion, aspirer, discoverer, visionary, home and God lover, true patriot or pathetic piece of crap?

He's the slime ball, not you--but never go back to him though, just like you always do.

Give me power to go on Father cuz I sure don't feel like it. What a shock life is on a daily basis.

The SRI's blocked all pattern recognition so I continued to mess up without ever any correction.

FRIEND

All other women can't believe you took a stand. Now they'll all follow suit and make this demand.

I want honest, smart and enthused workers. Attention to detail, quick and inventive learners.

Maxine Watters is totally corrupt putting down Trump but the dumbed liberals eat it all up.

They're too dumb to understand it anyway.

A disgusting spirit coming into your house.

If they're gonna act that way don't let them in your house and it's your kids who are the worst.

Another silent empire is dirty jokes—a dark spirit, trains children, bad demonic hold, being yoked.

You should never allow off-color jokes in your home. Disgusting, dark, unhappy, demons.

Everything has gotta be upright, above board, clearly seen, understood, decent and straight.

Liberals are emotional wasteland—kill your spirit, misunderstand, make presumptuous demands.

it's an interactional process that takes place, as an ethologist I want to document that and be precise.

All I want is privacy, routine, beautiful surroundings to do my work now. A mansion on acreage with a wall.

There must be some nice decent men.

FRIEND

What made me change so fast? You said the buzzwords and that changed everything/it's a blast.

Man starts off as a potential genius and visionary only to end up a pedophile whoremonger.

Why does a pedophile look scruffy grunge? Cuz he couldn't care less, he's a predator not a sponge.

Mankind's plunge into wickedness.

He betrayed and lied to me but I don't feel bad cuz I got God my Dad.

What is a spongegrunge, it's a sinner with a double life, a manipulator and lecher too in style.

When things change the man may regress into porn--the most common problem of the hour.

These men are so low they don't mind the dark/dank and are just predators every day and hour.

Disgusting lechers are dying vultures.

Flesh-eating spirit: ravenous, rapacious, depthless, can't get enough (young women) or anything else.

Man is duplicitous cuz he has two sides. We all do (a matter of control) but crookedness is despised.

The false churches justifying gay marriage and abortion: compromisers with the world, I hate em.

He's lower than a dirty rat, he's a slug.

He's the dross, you're the most.

FRIEND

Two sides: With fear or trauma he regresses to previously successful strategies like tantrums.

The whoremonger does many things right but don't get sidetracked and stay in the light.

Is this the man who made not God his idol of devotion?

It's been a nightmare knowing you, living in a junk pile too.

Women think if they have to take it, I gotta take it and anything else they're not having it.

Male alcoholic insults, pulls her down, mocks her looks. What's there left but to just get drunk?

Once you see the light there is no reason to wait.

The lady said "I hate his guts so much it makes me wretch".

Alcohol Psychosis: a broken record. The same argument for 30 years and can't forget it, ever.

Broken record is never worked through. Incompleted mourning, distracting, avoiding the truth.

Reliance on unreliable people is a form of being unequally yoked and it makes one so provoked.

Here you're paying/relying on them but your spirit is vexed and it becomes a big mal-adaptation.

Computers level playing field so I'm on par with you--even broke someone comes along enthused.

In God's timing is there ever delay? No, even if a year or decade, trust Him ok.

FRIEND

You have developed something or a way of thinking that no one else has. It's called style: *panache*.

Needing workers desperately puts you in a sick relationship with them so relax/pray for wisdom.

Oh! I get it. Whenever they say they can do it it means they *can't* do it.

All new crew is good for you--no confusion from the past/ now you know just what you want, too.

No projections/resentments from the past, all new crew/more streamlined too, now success finds you.

You work hard all your life and then you retire. Now you can finally think, create and be inspired.

Is there ever delay in God's timing? NO, and that's what you gotta know.

Home: Unless I own it I gotta deal with people and I can't stand it.

Take failure as sign you're close, a cluster of em = you're right on the cusp and next to be blessed.

Humiliating failure today can bring your win as it pushes you to the end.

Utter humiliating failure was the kick in the butt you needed to get over the finish line undefeated.

She did me wrong but wasn't smart enough to see it so my correction brought a really big jolt.

You can't make them smart, so suddenly you may be alone--but God will always provide that one.

FRIEND

It's called decompensation after the shock of reality disintegration.

I see it as a mal-adaptation. Yes it's generated from within as genetic potential but rolls out with friction.

The genetic potential to devolve like that into total madness was incremental, in steps.

I didn't have the tools/wisdom to deal with it so just devolved without any control over any of it.

Stress = genetic symptoms roll out.

Even if they did know what you were talking about they don't care--so best to wait for someone rare.

Way out of poverty: Finish high school, keep a job for one year, don't have children until marriage.

Relax then a moment comes when you can't help but begin--then take it through to the end.

It's not you it's anyone who wrecks my concentration--it doesn't matter who it is, it's interruption.

The longer the break the more it all comes together when you get back.

Take more breaks, get away from it. Regroup, toke, look at view, adjust attitude = complete it, whew.

It's right brain or left. Too much focus--get receptive then reverse back into the locus/the best.

Why do you think too much work makes Johnny a dull boy? It's the left brain, it's boring, it annoys.

FRIEND

Man has imagination and higher brain to do far more damage than animals even lions or snakes.

Go right brain cornucopia then return to work--with holy spirit ease it completes it all/you're first.

It's been proven over and again: If my attitude is right the work completes in itself in a second.

There's a line and you don't cross it. If you do, suddenly everything goes twit.

People can be lower than animals due to sinful evil and total depravity, two main Christian principals.

Nip it in the bud, stay away. Lookout for attacks from envy and jealousy.

The greatest punishment for sin comes from peoples' subliminal and automatic rejection of evil.

He who fights with monsters should be careful lest he thereby become a monster. Nietzsche

He's lazy, careless and passive. You don't need this from this plastic poser keeping you captive.

Find porn on his computer he's a adulterer cuz Jesus says it's all in the eyes/but not to fear.

Men are emotionally brittle so heed my guides: Man views porn, woman rejects, he suicides.

Pornography is a silent toxic empire and if you're yoked to someone who's into it you've had it.

He has led you to believe you need him for protection but he's the one you need protection from.

FRIEND

It's a form of insanity: the effects of pornography. Not just yelling but mistakes, faux pas, profanity.

Pornography means he's comparing them to you! And some women don't care, don't become blue?

If someone loses money he's a loser. If he's a careless procrastinator it aggravates like a boozer.

He won't let you have any money but also loses it honey while insisting you waste money.

He's a waster and a loser. A waster IS a loser. Holes in his bucket, imposture.

Outside of discipline is self-indulgence and decay.

The trouble I had crawling out of my shell for all those years--total resistances and many tears.

No one understood me/I didn't understand myself but fortunately I found Jesus who fixed the mess.

You'll only feel comfortable out of that system completely--maybe you should recognize that, see.

Must forgive all you've ever known. They didn't know, they were as dumb as you before growth.

If those hormones mean yelling at your wife you don't put up with it--look beyond surface/feminists.

Men who check out women in public have no respect for their wives. The suffering is deep like knives.

This silent empire in men's lives must be shattered for good cuz it's about brain chemicals/selfhood.

FRIEND

After years of preparation you will finally cross the great divide. This is a sudden change--oh my!

You've done the work now get ready for "overnight" success tho' you've been workin' forever miss.

You work and work and suddenly the spotlight's on you and that's how it works so relax for perks.

The most inspired are also the most susceptible to captivation by demons so watch out friends.

You enable this kind a thing, you're just as bad as that cad.

Women are so desensitized/divorced from their feelings and bodies they don't even care.

Stop shame that stops your work. You gotta come out, it was just demons causing those quirks.

What we're talking about here is the effect of brain hormones and I have to adapt to those?

Online porn is a past-time of most men and the sign is yelling at their wives. Nip it in the bud, thrive.

No wonder marriages fall apart/start bickering with these subtle messages going on--that's porn.

If 70% of Christian men are into pornography, no wonder I don't wanna go to church--demons lurk.

Once you forgive em now you can take the good from the bad experience, get greater and go on.

FRIEND

 Divine vindication is necessary for the relief of the saints. God gets the haters, since the ancients.

Bashed identity from apathy: lost steam, serenity and fascination with work God gave to thee.

Conservatives think like lions, liberals think like lambs.

Happy I never have to see you again. Tho' you robbed me I'm free to find new helpers and friends.

For that which is highly esteemed among men is abomination in the sight of God. Luke 16: 15

I don't care what it looks like, I believe that God is working.

You communicate thru a readily understandable image not by spouting off just to show your stuff.

It's about the copy not what I look like.

God loves seeing you fight the good fight, rejoicing and praising Him even when pricked by the knife.

I feel happy and free now I'm not unequally yoked to thee, it was terrible but now you're gone, whee!

I hated being dependent on you. You were dismissive, offputting, made me crazy too (so blue).

I can't walk with the wicked--the crooked, the double minded. Hooked to you was confinement.

Baby, the wicked like you with such poor character are easily recognized and they are everywhere.

FRIEND

Superior man can't be on the begging end cuz--unequally yoked--they will have power over him.

When interviewing workers you gotta use your intuition. This instinct will save you from destruction.

They just can't get it together, they can't see the whole. It's boring even trying, let God take control.

We want Christmas, Easter, town fairs and parades--it is sentimentality for the good ol' days.

Elder consciousness--saging--is more sedate, contemplative, pensive, creative and reclusive.

My function is to sit here 20 hours a day and do what I do while running the entire household too.

Rehabilitation: a leopard changing his spots?

I need solitude to bring it through.

He is now at a later stage in life, psychologically--more monastic, quieter, inward, universal.

You overcame so much, you went thru so much (God knows this) but after the pot is perfect it's over.

He uses your foes for discipline but when whole He turns on them worse so let that be the goal.

Remember it'll now be the opposite to all you known: fame not mocking, ridicule, rejection, scorn.

The past was just your lesson not life sentence so change your attitude to opportunities ahead.

FRIEND

Recalling past persecution takes you down to that location--like little anchors it pulls you down.

The person you knew at sixteen is not the same. It's another person so stop carrying that flame.

I'm not wasting time I'm regrouping and will be soaring.

Enjoy a walk, play ball with dogs, watch Bonanza, make some salsa, take a nap then watch the sunset.

The longer you wait the easier/faster it will complete.

It's "correct and firm" until the very end.

Don't work just get into that space where with holy spirit ease the whole thing completes itself: aced.

Deadlines are deadly so don't compulse just work on your receptivity to get it all done quickly.

Don't work--hold back strength--until that moment you cannot NOT work and you go to the end.

If you're just kind and attentive to animals you'll be amazed at the affection they will show you.

At last a coder who can replicate me the designer and I'm gonna party forever cuz he's so clever.

You'll never get a chance to tell me I'm doing it wrong/am a heretic cuz it's just Him and me: fantastic.

Open your perception to increasing opportunity in an abundant environment for you and me.

FRIEND

Cosmic: When finally whole (mature) everything comes into perfect order around the superior man.

Don't have to sell myself just read my words if you don't like em I don't care nor even know.

The mark of a brilliant teacher is how many don't come back.

To do your best work keep taking the day off. You will get so creative it will all finish itself.

This is for the delicate, the refined, the perspicacious, the fascinated, the sharp, the higher mind.

To do your best work just do what you want. You will want to work when sparked, that's my rant.

Don't come without calling. I don't like surprises cuz I have my own synchronicity/you ain't it.

I have nothing to brag about but daily assiduity and that's what brought me where I am today.

Every day even Sunday I arose at midnight and worked to the next night: a prepared mind is ready.

All sin creates insanity but with repentance the symptoms leave in a glorious return to normalcy.

Pornography has been minimized all this time but that's mainly liberals who debased us (slime).

Pornography a powerful yet unmentioned empire, a major focus, and it's hard to imagine this.

FRIEND

A rich life may be consolation for going to hell so don't envy prosperity or go under it's spell.

They know you/familiar with your habits. The bad ones make em hate you and the good won't make it up.

Why did it slip from consciousness? Because you adapted to it, no longer believe it or he denied it.

Women are coached to put up with this crap—pornography with men. That is bull my friends.

Porn is minimized by women—legitimized, justified, don't make waves, at least it's not a dame.

Christian forgiveness means to forget all the crap he did. It's what we came here to learn I guess.

I love hearing the crow in the morning and the crickets at night. I love my new home, outa the blight.

I don't do phones. I hate them with a passion and they give me headaches that last all day, ashen.

Phones are just a modern invention and people are obsessed with them: entry points for demons.

With email I can think about it/have a record of it, but phones are pure chaos and I'm thru with it.

Facetime, all that invasive stuff, it's none of your business what I look like, it's privacy vs. fluff.

Liberals think nothing of cutting corners constantly and they're corrupt—these aren't the old days.

FRIEND

So you go off the deep end every once in awhile--so what. That shows the deep emotions of poets.

Loftily, I don't laugh and chirp but have learned to just sit quietly and nod because civility comes first.

Tolerance of pornography comes from the liberal viewpoint which is: anything goes and it's appalling.

It helps to see it as an evil sex spirit rather than a slight to you but it still feels like hell being fooled.

Old fears determine perception. God help us all, we're living in a dream, a delusion. Get clear, son.

It's a silent empire and women are told to put up with it and man, that is the worst possible advice.

He's comparing her to you, he needs to see smut to get it up but are you kidding, forget that!

She was less than from adapting to him but when he recovered she was forgiving.

Society is a common code for self-restraint. Stefan Molyneux

Psalms 35-40 tells all about how He's gonna get that creep--it's so telling, wonderful and sweet.

I've developed an art of writing and speaking called telling the truth.

Sick youthist culture says the end is the worst--no, it's the best. So don't worry aging, it's your crest.

FRIEND

A complete psychotic loss of reality and attempted suicide all over a blink you shoulda taken in stride.

It's easy to go into denial if you're always busy--it's compartmentalization you see.

You must flush em out. Even if they gossip aboutcha, you see who they are so let out a shout.

He's the kinda person who will gossip out everything you send him, all so he can mightily grandstand.

That's Dan: he grandstands at your expense man.

Don't make him mad (don't poke a bear). Just skillfully navigate and then be glad he's not there.

Triangulation is strangulation. That's you talking behind my back with another: I'd block, censure, ban.

To rid yourself of painful remorse, think way into the future when no one remembers it or the source.

Going into denial is simple cuz i'm so busy anyway but then it erupts every once in awhile despite all.

It's a matter of being mad but ladylike.

I became prejudiced against all men suddenly, it was awful--see vindictive females, often unlawful.

Show them why your way is best.

One reaction to suicide is anger, bringing up crap from the past when he was young and dapper.

FRIEND

More important things than what you said or did. Get out of self to the proper perspective (put a lid).

Dogs dig but can be trained and people too can change and gain, in the main (not always, just sayin').

Most Americans suck at everything. We just muddle thru and hope for the best. Ben Shapiro

Do your work, leave a legacy, make some money, support a family--that's it, not your ego honey.

Please give me nylon granny panties from the fifties when things were comfortable, not these.

Get weak, fall into the popular groove (which is awful, stupid, destructive) so stay strong I behoove.

How stupid and inefficient: hip hugger panties. You have two waistbands, loved by trendies.

They've made us wear uncomfortable false-sexy low cut panties forever and we're sick of it--hear?

Whenever someone keeps telling you he's your friend, I don't know man.

It is tyrannical for you to have expectations of how I should act, that's just a consciousness fact.

Clothiers: Return from this uncomfy (irritating) hip-hugger tragedy to nylon granny panties, please.

Control of sensual desires is being a Christian soldier.

Music speakers: what is incredible with treble becomes lousy with bass, what is the answer boss?

FRIEND

Are you a legend to yourself or just hidden by God? Think: before that minute you're seen as odd.

They wanna pamper themselves but don't deserve it. Get off your fat ass and study, learn, order it.

You're the man's natural adversary if a feminist. You can't sacrifice, give, take second place/best.

Don't give me your fakery/false image. Do you work all day, stay orderly, take care of kids/dogs/cats?

It's Jesus plus nothing or else you're saying His death isn't enough to pay for your sins, see?

Your works are trash compared to what He did for us so just believe then you quickly progress.

No wonder men went to men, who would want this? Homosexuality & feminism were simultaneous.

When male-female relationships turn adversarial all hell breaks loose and explodes in your face.

For the system to work, be a sweet little lady and he'll become a manly provider with nothing shady.

Women have lost all attractiveness acting like this. It's magnetism vs. acting like a shrew or a bitch.

You demand respect cuz you can't command it—that'll never work cuz you're lazy and indulgent.

Men should wait to find a sweet little lady. Not give in to this feminist hex for sex then a hellish reality.

FRIEND

I feel so much better having transcended the female class which in this era is the classless ass.

Real women aren't offended cuz they know it's true. They had men friends but women they'd eschew.

Pornography is adultery. Jesus said it's all in the eyes baby.

It's what you click on that can change your life forever buddy and you lost a helluva lot, truly.

When women have the ontologically fatal insight that all you see is delusion and bull, it's hell.

One click and he lost everything, how amazing. Forgive but never forget, now he makes you sick.

You trusted, you forgave. Again betrayed you forgave but never have to see his face again I say.

It's that click that makes you a filthy hick and we see that now, heck--we're brought down by your hex.

What hurts so much is him comparing them (that) to you. He can't see this/thinks it's trivial too.

You're one click away from hell buddy. No saying "I knew it was clickbait, nothing there, really!"

You "have no idea what I'm talking about" and you didn't try to find out so forget you too, caio!

Bold and the Beautiful gives me courage to turn on the savage cuz after she cheated Liam did it.

FRIEND

Please Lord make me rich and famous so I no longer have to put up with this.

The farmer waits expectantly for precious harvest from the land, keeping vigil until it rains. James 1: 7

It's whatcha call a pre-success crisis, a terrible and sudden turn of events.

You're disloyal and wavering with divided interests so purify your hearts of spiritual adultery. James 4:8

Doesn't matter what he says, it's what he does, especially when you're not looking or distracted.

You have such low standards and I such high standards, sorry we can't get it together friend fairweather.

"Oh, he's sick"--give me a break! What we're talking about is a filthy hick and to infinity it stinks.

On pornography: You must hate it and eloquently state it. It's not Christian to put yourself in temptations way, teasing it.

It's easier to sin on computers but also easier to get the proof.

Porn is a terrible problem largely ignored while the devil's bitten then you're carried away, smitten.

If he wants to look at dirty pictures, get another.

It wasn't God that brought this temptation but the individual's own evil desires and passions.

I live in community that takes care of my business and emergencies--more important than family.

FRIEND

The inveterate sinner becomes a nameless faceless creature to you--someone you used to know.

I hate even talking about this but it was brought into my midst and boy am I pist at this sudden twist.

What hurts your stomach girl is unconscious recognitions.

He that justifies the wicked, that's the kinda thing I'm sick of.

Never speak to them again: those who justify wicked men.

The lady said "he said he didn't do it so we went back together, it was just a buildup of gossip".

My mom isn't around to tell me not to talk the way I do, whew

It wasn't that he lied--he saw the signs then filled in the filthy lower archetype.

The fact that "all men do it"--is that supposed to make her feel better? Not on your life, ever.

He doesn't want you to "air our dirty laundry"--of course he says that honey.

He's had the devil in him since the day he was born but just learned to hide it better, forget him.

He says "it's no big thing"--just that's enough you know about him.

It's the little foxes that kill the vine and clicks that bring ruin and decline.

Peace and prosperity then sudden destruction.

The destruction would not have been what it was were it not for a recurrent pattern of this scuzz.

FRIEND

 Don't trust him if he's nice. Learn to see past images he portrays which are often a device.

When opprobrium comes back to bite you in the butt cuz you screwed up recall you chose this route.

Though it was just a straw breaking the camel's back her whole world went black, that's a fact.

He went right back to it like a dog returning to it's vomit.

Pornography is of the devil cuz he always gets you thru the sensual level.

Where is your line? Make it be pornography, adultery of the mind.

Is your beautiful house and yard filled with decrepitude and thorns cuz he's lazy and into porn?

You need a team you can trust no more being crushed--walk away, you must.

But man, with all his honor and pomp, does not remain: he is like the beasts that perish. Psalm 49:12

No brag, just fact.

Fortune favors the bold.

The lady said "Am I seeing things, am I hearing things--am I crazy or is he? Forgive me if it's me".

Learn to see past images. Man has two sides and we all have a tiger inside, don't take it in stride.

They never wanna judge anyone so call it a "pathology of the ghetto" or "all men do it you know."

FRIEND

To maintain a home is not just to clean it but to keep stuff out of it.

Sensual sins manifest in disorder: in looks, thoughts, environment, not being in the moment.

Don't get complacent. Keep working/talking.

This archetype you're playing out has about run out. It's old, pat, mediocre and boring as well.

The mature male is whole which is a charming integration of a developed anima and animus.

The mature male has a fully developed female side but the male dominates and this is greatness.

Neurotics over-rely on the verbal.

We can't go back, so bye.

No matter what you got, trouble may come so live for the best and pray it won't and enjoy your night.

It's much better for you to pull back rather than rush forward saying "it is me", let Me do it said He.

An unstable mate is like the death by a thousand cuts, you're in a rut with a sick feeling in your gut.

He will go to the generation of his fathers, who will never more see the light. Psalms 49: 19

A man who is held in honor and understands not is like the beasts that perish. Psalms 49: 20

FRIEND

Don't be a hick, wait for the click then everything is suddenly done and nothing is left undone.

Wait to work, when you want to. Then it's like pulling a string in a sweater, it all pulls through.

A complex personality is like a multifaceted diamond but what if one side is black? It destroys/brings lack.

There is always a pre-success crisis before pay dirt. Like husband landing in the hospital, or worse.

What hurts so much is the ontologically fatal insight that your reality is wrong, ridiculous, shot, NOT!

He cannot live there and have prurient interests, be a total Calvinist--that means decency first.

I don't wanna go to any more parties, please. It's always their opportunity to zing me from jealousies.

I'm waiting for the click in my head when with holy spirit ease the whole project completes itself.

I haven't had that click in the head yet when everything makes sense in a split second.

You're a fool to work without that click in your head when instead of stressful labor, you spring ahead.

It'll all just come together, nothing missing and perfect instantly.

Read Psalms 35-40: savor like fine wine cuz every word is a gold mine.

LIBERAL

What's happened to people? A dumbing down by design, from a false cosmology crossing the line.

"All men created equal" was what Jefferson said to England for separation not what *they're* sayin'.

Liberal millennials spit in your face and though it's all arrested development it's no less disgrace.

Leftism gets extreme: with time they kill the cream then murder more--not enough equality it seems.

Tell everyone you're doing bad or else they will steal from you. --Russian socialism survivor.

Just as women are not equal to men, not all men are equal to each other.

Diversity creates strife not strength.

Best argument against democracy: a five minute conversation with the average voter. Churchill

The marching feminists engaged in naughty behavior dressed like vaginas and humping each other.

Most absurd myth of all history: women part of combat in the military.

Because of our milder more refined natures we're being pushed into the periphery like lepers.

LIBERAL

If you listen to fake news I'm gonna know it.

What makes the world go 'round is men willing to stand up against scum. Alex Jones

Liberal collectivism is an unmitigated nightmare but we're free, individuals, unique and rare.

Reckless overuse: When everything is racist, nothing is. Tucker Carlson

Obama lied to us eloquently. Trump tells the truth crudely. Mary Harris

We didn't steal it from Indians they were always killing each other and our cavalry was a barrier.

Oprah "cares for women" but not those in slave factories or sterilized in Africa by her operation.

California declines into a third world renter state with small towns crushed by criminals' escape.

The dems can't win a debate so use population replacement to seem great.

Obama a smooth-talker, a hustler and a nation-killer. But you loved him and still do, what a joker!

The problem with silly women is they love big government: globalism, open borders and Oprah.

Oprah opens old wounds of whites killing blacks in 1950 but never about her friend the devil Harvey.

Why are women the reason for this mess? Because they love big gov and open borders sis.

LIBERAL

A true artist must be mature intellectually or he'll be wanting approval and conforming to the rabble.

You can't reason people out of a position if they haven't been reasoned into it. By rote they learned it.

They chirp, mingle, coo, smile, laugh at pointless jokes--the social arena, an unequal yoke.

Liberals: the ones who say "let em all in" are the ones who can afford to live away from them.

People who have moved to the least diverse areas are the ones most in favor of diversity, no fear.

Don't envy the wicked when they prosper cuz they'll be mowed down like the grass in one hour.

The American dream is alive for those unversed in the ideology of victimhood. Thomas Sowell

Oprah speaks of "the courage of women" as if men aren't the same species always hurting the darlings.

"Trump is Hitler and will commit genocide". Barrack Obama at the peak of his insanity and pride.

Why admire those who give up their gifts and talents when young thru a nasty pursuit of hedonism?

Oprah and Meryl saying men are bad but then defend a child rapist and you're still on board? Sad.

You're not a true artist if you're virtue signaling on trendy topics--that's cheap, easy and garbage.

LIBERAL

Better mature a little before putting out crap like that. The clear will see it and rat/you'll go splat.

The neurotic liberal is too wimpy to ever tell the truth to a crowd of the dumbed down or blue.

Go ahead and virtue signal all you want. Put your dull stuff out there to be loved, but you won't.

I wouldn't post, publish or perform until you get outa you echo chamber of deviants from the norm.

Your worst enemies will encourage you to do wrong--those "friends" from the liberal throng.

You make your conclusions first then try to shoehorn your findings to fit—not good work/not legit.

Oprah sells magical thinkin' to disempowered women sitting home watching television desperate for livin'.

You don't harm innocence without massive, biblical, catastrophic wrath as a consequence.

Oprah pushed monster Obama, as part of a secret deep state government cabal in America.

Oprah manages "Me Too" movement where Trump is bigot not Hollywood for which she's front.

To see Hollywood scum hang on her every word you'd think Oprah was God and to be preferred.

Reason brings individualism and brainwash brings collectivism. Why: as individuals we can reason.

LIBERAL

Swedish feminists applauding gang rapists are the biggest example/proof liberalism is a mental illness.

Dumber people are more violent. That's why we gotta use your wits to hold em down or we've had it.

Turgid political correctness makes us feel blocked, depressed, hopeless but God'll reverse this mess.

The thing I hate most about liberals is their darn complacency with these people out to get us.

The devil's crowd is attracted to the spin but God's men are individuals and repent of sin.

They say "they can do it" when they can't (Dunning-Kruger Effect)--best to assume they're all full of it.

Liberalism is a mental illness and must be approached as one--it's not just ornery wives or the brattish

The stronger we get with Donald Trump the more evil erupts--democrats just can't give it up.

They cut from Oprah who "helps women" to Meryl Streep who defends a child rapist and pedophilia.

It's too much, either we're all gonna be dead or like Nineveh we'll return from the brink, glad.

Hillary is hunchback evil and twisted but Oprah's still got that shining light leading us hellbent.

Christian persecution happens in many ways. From being disinvited to genocide or loss of pay.

LIBERAL

They use to seek out the elderly for keys of wisdom. Not anymore, they have all the answers.

Why should you adapt to your kid's perversions just cuz he learned em in school? This is so uncool!

The liberal hypocrisy made me sick. He dared turn the spot light on me when he's ok turning trix?

I don't wanna enter that cold realm again, a liberal phony thing.

Of course the Manual is conservative--to balance out the leftist crap we've been a prisoner of.

You trying to force me to accept this nasty thing and now imposing it on kindergarten children?

50's showed normal conflicts in the home like jealousy/procrastination, now it's sexual bedlam.

Puritans were disgusted with debauchery and that was the chaste mindset which began America.

The "gay community" gets filthier, edgier, more in your face-ier and it's a Hollywood gay mafia.

Don't go that way unless you wanna die at 42.

America began as Puritanism and that's what freedom's dependent upon. You sin you lose it hon'

A trash-filled crap hole describes the home of the porn addict and his poor wife who puts up with it.

Why would impotent old men get into porn? Cuz they're weak and evil is how they were born.

LIBERAL

 New technology means everyone is famous. They have their own red carpets, aren't they marvelous.

They're so dumb they think "progressive" means they're intellectuals, modern, chic, with-it.

It's ok to be white.

Get rid of all of famous white man statues and replace them with statues of convicted crack addicts.

Oprah attacks all men but not Harvey Weinstein who she pimped for and openly sucked ear of.

Save yourself incredible time/energy. Anyone hating Trump doesn't deserve your thoughts honey.

How could anyone hate Trump after all he's done for us, especially saving us from Europe's mess?

If not for Trump we'd be flooded with people seeking to conquer us, but you hate him? Ridiculous.

The devil's crowd is too weak to stand for truth. They just slide in with the majority/are bores too.

They're all wrong, as a group. You're right on, as an individual lover of goodness and truth.

True intelligence or just virtue signaling to be loved by the majority? "Progressive" is a human tragedy.

Renaissance is the flowering of uniqueness. Superior men to the center as we're rid of "progressives".

God gave us a wonderful barometer of good vs evil: it was Donald Trump or Hillary the devil.

LIBERAL

Not only do non-geniuses get spotlight, now know-nothing females are spouting off about life.

Having very little to say they say it constantly.

They take advice from their own ilk--an echo chamber of liberal ideas we've all had to gulp.

The correct thought, the approved mindthink: this explains it all I guess, not that people are finks.

Any kind of depth or circuitous novel reasoning brings their panic--a schooled reaction to genius.

You don't understand: it's the contagion of madness keeping you down so now break the connection.

They deny reality, attack the honorable, slander the competent and scorn the knowledgeable.

With Christianity gone there's a value vacuum and in rushes socialism.

Oprah's of the Great Society from the 60's where black illegitimacy went from 5% to this 80% spree.

Ask yourself why you're impressed with them--their outward spin or thinking they're so in?

Through the contagion of madness cultures go down together but God's men hold to faith sir.

Big fanfare, a rare event, then nothing. That's the way of the heathen who don't know eternity.

Americans are breaking free of worshipping elitism: royalty, red carpet and Hollywood, the Clintons.

LIBERAL

You got the sickening facts, now tell the world how they've been axed, kill heroes/be an iconoclast.

I'll never forget how you *loved* Obama and *loved* Hillary and when she lost you sobbed, crazy.

Obama was about surface polish, glibness, niceness, *image*. Speak nice to hide vice, voted in twice.

You loved the world's/history's worst criminals, biggest heist of all time, killing/displacing millions.

You were so stupid couldn't see through Clintons or Obama--wooed by cool image in charge of ya.

Oprah is a globalist operative, a front who reads off a script and you're a fan thinking she's legit?

No more debauched elites but rather Americana, what we produce, the common man and woman.

Dems turning against the Clintons marks a new stage as Hollywood collapses: backlash, rage.

Sold us out! Sold our booty to enemies, cashing in: that was Obama and Clinton and you loved em?

Oprah brought honey to sweetheart Harvey who's just as twisted as her: Hollywood scum lovelies.

Sex talk: ban em from your circle. Return to Puritanism as America began when pure not miserable.

What is the most telling thing about this debauched generation? Women into/tolerating porn.

LIBERAL

How could you paste a rainbow over your child's face? Are you crazy, do you want him that way?

See it as a Gay Mafia: one word against perversion and they'll sock ya but now we're above ya.

Conceit/arrogance of coastal liberals looking down on bitter clinging God-lovers in the center.

How liberals float our boat: massive regulations and overspending on anything for the vote.

Giving away free stuff for votes is very expensive. That's what happened in California, extensive.

All they do is take selfies--thousands! Think of what this means as it all goes to hell it seems.

If they have a rainbow superimposed on their child's face you know they're the lowest creepy case.

Why does "gayness" increasingly include pedophilia, pederasty, bestiality? Cuz it's plain nasty.

Gay is another word for pan sexuality: sex with anything, really.

Oprah Winfrey will never be president cuz she stuck her tongue in Weinstein's ear. Alex Jones

Haha your heroes are about to fall. Barry O., Hillary and all their cronies who are mostly pedophiles.

Fake Christians virtue signaling over the poor homos. They know nothing just repeat slogans.

They're not nasty? Haha Go to a Gay Pride Parade someday.

LIBERAL

Oprah sucked Harvey's ear and baited women to be raped by this character.

Don't try to understand it, keep your nose out of it. Don't sink so low cuz it's just sin, garbage: satanic.

Just cuz something's common now we're supposed to excuse it? That's got nothing to do with it.

What used to be a "sin" is now a "sickness". What a cop out man, repent of your desires and filthiness.

It used to be a filthy sinner was shamed straight. Nowadays he's just "sick" so we should congratulate.

Stop counseling me if you're just following the herd which justifies sins by calling it preferred.

Oh, the poor guy--he's a pedophile! That's a sickness so let's coddle him and make him feel in style.

You will come out of this terrible time into the light of day, happy again, and it's all about sin.

Pedophilia is pandemic so that makes it more right than it was--if the herd's into something, so what.

Oprah is the "good club" and her phony world religion is only there to help by decreasing the pop.

Whenever liberals fail miserably they always say they didn't do enough and madly spend for stuff.

They'll use your money for their voters or you're a racist homophobe misogynist pig: haters.

LIBERAL

       They chirp, pander, bow, smile, suckup, look up, gossip. That's the herd man and he's toxic.

The opportunists hide behind humanism. That is an old trick and we don't have to accept it man.

The politician is silver tongued whether from a teleprompter or off the cuff and it's usually guff.

Obama got the Nobel Peace Prize for dropping 100,000 bombs/drones on 7 countries in 8 years.

Obama was constantly at war but we were led to believe he was a dove.
Yes it's a sickness and it comes from Satan who's into this.

The world's gone crazy filled with pedophiles it's like a new style and it's Satanic elitism of devils.

You think you know so much you spoiled arrogant creep? You're gonna fall cuz it isn't Me you seek.

Don't blame yourself, you took the filthy culture on. What happens when anyone swims in mud?

Look at what the dirty democrats have done to us. For years we've put up with this, decades of dung.

They've slid into hell, no longer the labor mass with true concern for common man or middle class.

They're complacent cuz they haven't been challenged, but once they are they'll fight, reengaged.

The more they virtue-signal, more they do the opposite as a male feminist becomes a rapist/sadist.

LIBERAL

Unless there is Christian character there are weird invasive encroachments and dumb mistakes.

Agree on price then they add more on it. I don't mind paying more but can't stand encroachment.

Poor character will show in their work. Nip it in the bud, shirk.

If they bait and switch, if requirements are too confusing, if they disappear, if they call you dear...

Learn to read the small signs of disrespect, bait and switch, fudging or the Dunning Kruger effect.

Watching for Christian character vs. all the other it will be easy to sift through all the bidders.

I see it all the time with animal-lovers: Always virtue signal about it but then are worst abusers.

They're now really dirty cuz moral relativism brought all hell out into the open creating Bedlam.

They hate him because he's making America great again? Those aren't your friends!

They're teaching men not to be assertive and women to be basket-cases--it's all declassified.

We should be thanking God for Donald Trump or Hillary woulda let em ALL in-- millions!

Shield your children from toxic Academia.

They're judging the moral content of our character by collective concepts like race and gender.

LIBERAL

The globalists picked and groomed Oprah as a Judas goat, a smiling black face to slit your throat.

When you meet Trump haters say "but he's making America greater" and now you'll see the traitors.

Disturb any women's party by saying you love Trump and detest Oprah as crud and globalist front.

It's so easy for "angel" Oprah to recall the past when a black was killed by a white person in America.

If the west is destroyed, women's rights are too--but feminists don't question that as a rule.

It was the treachery of women leading to the downfall of the west where they are treated the best.

It was "emperor worship" until Christianity called it bad. Think of that: why they want us dead.

Fall of Rome: rising lawlessness, lack of discipline and growing bureaucracies.

Rome: Loss of respect for tradition, degradation of young and decline of art/entertainment/rhetoric.

Just like in America, falling Rome's intellectuals said "your traditions and ancestors were bad".

Falling Rome decayed, becoming selfish and lazy but like the west, pathologically self-critical.

We learn self-discipline or there are disasters--but when the state fixes it we degrade much faster.

Like falling Rome, a shift in who's popular: athletes, singers, actors who please the senses, eyes, ears.

LIBERAL

You are the children of heroes but only heroes get to keep their freedoms, not you weirdos.

The divide is so great if you have liberals in family you just gotta separate. Enmeshed = mean fate.

In ancient Rome, female influence in politics brought decline then foreign invaders took everything.

Roman feminism brought decline then foreign invasion spelled the end of them, they died.

With wealth and opportunity in the last thirty years, women's happiness has declined. Wonder why?

Wealth and power gets lazy: pessimism, frivolity, hedonism, materialism, decline of religion.

A decline of religion brings decline in virtue and I can sure see this, can't you?

The feminists for Hillary were fat and stodgy in their refusal to debate—they'd just ban, censure, hate.

Even with obvious dangers they don't save civilization because at this point, why bother?

If you feel you are descendants from evil you see no civilization to defend.

Women have become dirty. Flipping the bird, using the F-word, fat and loose, who'd wanna seduce?

Stats show the youth are not interested in God or Jesus. We're a post-Christian society and I fear it.

Diseugenics: the degeneration of bloodlines. Compare to fifty's females who were slim, trim and nice.

LIBERAL

It's liberalism that is a mental illness and feminism is the worst part of this while men are wimps.

Dictatorial female tyrants controlling people through gossip and social control--yes, they do that.

Compare em to fifty's women--like night and day. Don't you want a little lady not this weird decay?

Demanding respect, questioning, arguing, complaining, ridiculing, loving dangerous creeps.

They're so blatantly wrong in everything they think and say and bring in people who hate the gays.

These phony feminists open borders to the biggest misogynists the world's ever witnessed.

I'm not putting down women but feminism in them, a demon that makes them unhappy and unlovin'.

They're such shallow thinkers it's totally group-determined. Groupthink is a stink and women are finks.

When a weak woman's in power, watch out. They haven't had centuries of leading that tempers it.

Women love the idea of socialism, government expansion, open borders to everyone = we're ruined.

Once women suck off government it can manipulate half the pop but you can't see that can you broad.

Females see government as daddy/husband both, loving Hillary/doesn't matter what she does.

LIBERAL

Men are nationalists, best for self-interest. But women don't mind dealing with bureaucrats officious.

I pray that the demon of feminism is removed from your system including phony feminist men.

Women want a strong man for protection but become vicious with wimps who are not predilected.

They hate men who've fallen off the pedestal. Watch out cuz this can get horrible, she's not adorable.

If women aren't lil' ladies respectful of men, it's like letter a pit viper outa her cage and its mayhem.

If momma's not happy, no one's happy. Everyone knows that but that's not the way it should be.

Everything they say--and make everyone agree with--is pure bull. It's just ideology, theory, delusion, nil.

I am responsible for the climate change so I gotta pay the rich elites for my carbon usage.

Feminists seem like dazed zombies but we're into science, God, universe-- amazed as we can be.

Big, fat, thick as brick, sarcastic, caustic but she's so slow, not quick, dishes are stacked up.

She's above housework, too good for it--so those tasks passed down are now just negligence.

Divorce or having affairs is chic to this clique. It's too high a cost when trust is lost/it can't be fixed.

LIBERAL

Marriage gives you a life. Being single sux yet feminists seek their freedom tho' find only strife.

Since they don't know anything but slogans, of course they see conspiracy theories as no value, none.

To even argue with them is so defeating, energy depleting-- for they're never conceding believe me.

They can't think deeply. If you challenge them they walk away, censure, ban, see you as creepy.

Simultaneously, democrats destroyed our cities--all liberal strongholds, broke and filthy.

Dumb love war. Smart learn from history, don't go there--inbred imbeciles are nihilistic, a scare.

A mature female looks back at feminist past with embarrassment and anguish, astonished.

Having bought into feminist views she regresses into a cesspool causing mental illness too.

The only thing good is our own inner journey to God and leaving the rest to our great president Trump.

We elected him, that was our greatest achievement. Now enjoy your freedom/reap the benefits.

If Hillary'd gotten in we'd be flooded with immigrants in our streets, parks, counsels and houses.

It's all for votes and democrats don't care what it does to regular folks--like Merkel, it's adjust or else.

LIBERAL

I want him mean to my enemies, not me. That's a real man but feminists fear it makes em less free.

Men have been purposely wimped so we'd have no defense. Without men to protect us, we're dead!

Stop saying women can protect us--that's a bunch of bull! Get real, the world is laughing at us now.

Sorry that even tho' you wakeup to tattoos now you're permanently covered in black and blue.

Dear God it looks so ugly--a beautiful woman in an evening dress singing, covered in tattoos, beaming.

Overthrow decency, success, beauty, honor: desecrate and blaspheme it all.

Tattooed freaks have polyps of ink inside--colored tumors, bonafide.

Body piercings and tattoos mark a failing society filled with occult, blasphemy, false ideologies.

Bible portrays ugly societies filled with monsters/freaks and God said Kill em all even crops, please

Beautiful women ruined by black and blue tattoos become addicted, for then they want more too.

Go ahead, mark your bodies up, forget the future or thinking things through just join the club.

Charlie Manson was all for world government and killing/making us poor and promoted race wars.

It's nothing but the French Revolution and Jacobin: Sacrifice the rich for the good of everyone.

LIBERAL

Doublethink is holding two contradictory beliefs simultaneously and accepting both of them.

Seeking nirvana had a dark underbelly and it's the mental illness of liberalism culminating today.

Contend, O Lord, with those who contend with me and fight those who fight against me! Psalms 35

For some women "pure at heart" means putting up with stuff.

To love him you must be in denial. How sad the female brain must live in contradiction for survival.

When it comes to love no one's smart. The unbearable sorrows make us erratic, lethal and hard.

She's the type who won't celebrate Christmas cuz it will offend someone-- "many paths" she cons.

Due to the conflagratory nature of social hypnotism, the new tidal wave is definitely anti-Christian.

Weird personality distortions with repressed anger, which everyone has--a bunch of monsters.

You must trust, love and forgive spouse again: i.e. go back into denial like there was never a sin.

The hippie culture including Manson was French Revolution 1, now we see French Revolution 2.

Feminists responded to the mass molestation of women by giving flowers at the migrant center.

LIBERAL

They say will do something, then won't. Make promises/call you dear--no fear--then choke/revolt/float.

From now on it's the most serious, focused, clear, reliable workers with attention to detail, or bust.

Don't need to be asked twice, see what needs to be done, carries through and no pilfering hon'

Once that Christian work ethic based on true character is gone, life becomes hellish in the nation.

First they agree Jesus is Son of God then they say He's no better than Buddha, Krishna or an elf.

The more a man calls himself a "feminist" the sooner you can start the clock on rape charges. Milo

College gives you the right attitude towards minorities and the means to live as far apart as possible.

They start putting down family as birds of a feather: a nation without fathers or mothers.

Female culture: it was obvious I couldn't say a thing and not step on toes, that's liberal you know.

Liberals virtue signal all day because they have no virtue.

Virtue signaling marks the liberal. They are so maudlin about it too, half the world is starving you fool.

Men talk about politics, women virtue signal (that's intellectual) while shunning dissidents.

Migrant-welcomers are retarded nations led by virtue signalers intent on self-destruction.

LIBERAL

Success is the flourishing of peculiarity.

You can't adapt to them (petty). You must have your own circles around you (smart, strong, ready).

It's kind of a lark hearing them talk. Just sit silently and watch, listen, learn but when asked, opt out.

Female gabfests is petty stuff/chirping the accepted view. Thinkers stay silent or face the shrews.

Female culture is a severe block to feminine genius. Stay with the godly men, they will love us.

Female culture is petty stuff and the accepted view and every generation has different ones too.

You don't hate her you hate the feminism IN her--get that straight--but it is hard to get over.

The whining witch thing, the letting herself go love me anyways thing, the peremptory thing.

Demanding her needs be met, rolling them out, putting herself first, it's all such a turnoff miss.

Her job is to open the portals of mens' minds and create the environment for that to unwind.

Oprah brought women to Weinstein to be abused and about this filthy female you're so enthused?

Hollywood's hot pedophilic devil worshipper Oprah says it's the persecuted abused woman, poor her.

LIBERAL

Pushing the narrative that blacks are victims when in truth it's a Tsunami of black on white violence.

White racism is the greatest lie of our generation.

The Dunning-Kruger Effect: The incompetent can't know competence says our Donald Trump.

All those off-putting tattoos now letting her girl become a boy. Permanent mistakes and no joy.

Unruly teenagers, "reckless children" they call them, are violent mobs and a horrible problem.

We are not to mark up our bodies like the heathen do. You'll do anything to join the club won't you.

Esoteric Christianity came from Hippies and now every weird thing.

It's wonderful to see a youth unpeel the false self from all this stuff. Just become real, no more fluff.

Many trannies committing suicide--of course, why wouldn't they.

Given the choice of gender of course kids will make wrong decisions. Too many choices hon'.

How about loving being female but with male characteristics of logic and reason--that's integration.

Ellen hates Donald because he's white. What a racist: "not what we've learned to expect", what?

Both Charlie Manson and the Clintons rooted in hippyism.

You stayed with me for the "solitude" then brought your friends, lovers and brothers over dude.

LIBERAL

The kids love tyranny but tempered power only comes with maturity, so fear them in control, truly.

Why pay tuition if it means your destruction?

They just wanna upset the apple cart that's all. They're immature/don't know history at all.

Paying so your kids can put you and your way of life down--making the prince seem like a clown.

There's got to be conservative colleges to send them to. Don't be a fool where perverts' called cool.

The public is stampeding to the right just as the leaders are stampeding to the left. Douglas Murray

Fems: Either they use false ethics to gain power or they just don't have the information of the hour.

Mankind has lost all finesse-they've gone nuts. Recall the old days of grace, delicacy, elegance.

When it ruled Germany, women were best Nazis. When it ruled Russia, women the best communists.

Think of this when you recall the of terrible tyrants: women were the best Nazis and communists.

Virtue signaling and pathological altruism go together and we see it in women, the unclever.

Radical left is not driven by logic but emotion. Being a hypocrite is meaningless, just the revolution.

LIBERAL

To be famous with peers they virtue signal on trendy topics and make complete asses of themselves.

Dunning-Kruger Effect: Dummies thinking they're so smart, intellectuals--embarrassing to the Elect.

Your stupid book is just virtue signaling on trendy topics and putting down your religion and parents.

Silly feminists are big on putting down parents, even recalling made-up rapes and other events.

Logic and reason doesn't work on modern progressives--only shrill emotion and unforgiveness.

We could always return from the brink as in Nineveh, but unlikely since no repentance from any of ya.

Global stress is making people more sinful, not repentant, which is required for God's reprieve.

As to your puerile sloganistic opinions--you're of no value to us, we have evolved beyond thank God.

Just go on with your stupid book, like you're so important (all about you) but what about the world too?

What they write about is so puerile/personal and yet due to the Dunning-Kruger effect, it's the "all".

The famous feminist says she's 100% there on abortion--instantly she has no value: demotion.

Like women mimicking Betty Davis/Joan Crawford and falling flat on their face: just be yourself (ace).

LIBERAL

Whites just wanna be left alone—they're not attacking anybody but are themselves slaughtered daily.

The whole world is now targeting whites. Colonialism is their only known history and they wanna fight.

The liberals are heartless especially the youth—callous, negligent, uncouth/open borders too.

Black victim thing is a scam covering the tsunami of black-on-white crime so don't give me that.

The famous feminist "100% there" on abortion is not an "intellectual" but a heartless sadist.

Weak women in power are the most sadistic of all. Feeling deprived for centuries = most despicable.

They're actually heartless masochists who become sadistic. It's all virtue signaling/very narcissistic.

Just look at the blah blah after terroristic events of Theresa Mae, a virtue signaling liberal dame.

Camille Paglia is "100% there" with abortion and now she goes into the anals of history. Hah

So much for famous feminists who are composites of the worst ideas and attitudes of this curse.

Famous feminists have no heart. Or else they couldn't be spouting this crap/be democrats for a start.

Famous feminists are sadists, think of that.

Once women become "emancipated" the decline of the family is accelerated.

LIBERAL

You can have a feminized society but it won't survive Islam.

Multiculturalism means different attitudes towards cleanliness, punctuality, noise, pets, sex.

The main driver for the rise of high civilization is the degree of chastity of it's women. J.D. Unwin

There's a high correlation between the cultural achievement of a people and their sexual restraint.

As soon as society opens itself to sexual immorality it loses it's cohesion, impetus and purpose.

A nation full of happy families with longevity have "expansive energy" to influence others to prosperity.

Failure of feminism brought on Islamic invasion.

We've never seen a successful feminist society save short spans at the *end* of great empires.

SJWs play the Marxian game of dividing worlds into oppressor/oppressed with victim mentality.

It is a catastrophic Islamic invasion from misplaced compassion and hyper-emotionalism.

Feminist leaders will bring down gender inclusion of the west, replaced by hypermasculinity/tribalism.

It's shocking how women voted for Hillary cuz she was female. Can you imagine how shallow?

Oprah wants to save women from the "great evil" of Trump when she's the most anti-female block.

LIBERAL

Instead of addressing concerns of the people, leftists smear and morally grandstand supporting evil.

The liberal tactic of branding people with smear labels for social control has totally failed.

Oprah is the front for women to delete husbands and be wards of the state-- she's not love but hate.

They hated everything about America: the old hippies and their progeny--a tribe we wanna go away.

Godless spirituality: cults, paganism, witchcraft, psychic, reincarnation, astrology, parapsychology.

They are experts in non-answers/hide. They just never answer the question, slip and slide.

No matter what the problem is, they "find the bigot". That's the prism of perception throughout.

The smart people are bored with repetition but the dumbed feel real security in silly slogans.

Graduates of gender studies are dumber than when they started, being told weird things psychotic.

Feminism isn't about women, they're being used as a tool for central planning and collectivism.

"Identitarian authoritarians" are the worst fascists cuz we can't help it and America's sick of it.

Telling them what they wanna hear, provide excuses for failure, protect em from novel opinions.

LIBERAL

Virtue signaling is a mental illness cuz it prevents the signaler from seeing how he's killing the rest.

"We'll have no more racial strife when everyone's brown" but wait—diversity means dumb.

I don't want to accept alien ways of life. Attitude towards women, do they love God, how they treat dogs.

They put you down as a clown but later when it costs nothing they too jump on the bandwagon.

Draw out the spear and close up the way of those who pursue and persecute me. Say: it is I.

Feminists created the tragedy of population substitution by immorality like abortion and lesbianism.

Only hetero longerm marriages build strong lasting societies so feminists are the reason ladies.

Feminists destroyed the west, us and their own families. Many have left their own children, incredibly.

Dumbed women going along with feminism to toot their horn have no idea how they're about to mourn.

Obama lovers' uncritical conformity to the rot that came before Trump, redeeming barbarism.

They have particularist desires not universal principals.

Hegemonic belief systems are always invisible to those inside of them. Moses Apostaticus

Biggest myth of all time: "Nationalism is not Christian"--not true, we love strict borders and lines.

LIBERAL

When you lose your identity, as in a culture, you lose your will to survive.

Everything--history, family, culture, life--is less important than the cheap high of virtue signaling.

The west put women on a pedestal and now that's all being torn down.

"Overcome Islamic terrorism with openness and respect" or "if you kill your enemy, he wins". Justin Trudeau

How easily Hillary-lovers become scammers it's just their DNA learned from their masters.

Groupcentric urges--loyalty to in-group, hostility to out-group--seen in family or neighborhood.

Liberals embrace promiscuity and ever-earlier sex-education for their children--real perverts, man.

Liberals support single parenting, the bedrock of female poverty.

What does it say that he loves Hillary and Barrack? It says he's a pervert, a criminal and barbaric.

How we love our POTUS and how grateful we are to be saved from the rest of the world's predicament.

If Hillary'd gotten in we'd be swarmed with foreigners who wanna kill us and you love this witch?

Borders against pests: If they're in your city they'll be in your yard, house or neighborhood next.

Liberals are not about in-group loyalty: patriotism. They're against self-defense/wanna ban guns.

LIBERAL

Church is not supposed to reflect society but hold it's ground (by the book) or become crooked.

Liberals hate hierarchy cuz they can't compete, so they invite immigrants to take down elites.

How can the phony wimps of today ever defend us? We need real men, Americana men, Godly men!

Liberals are so stupid they think we should disband the military--like the whole world's friendly.

The same liberals who won't defend you also scam you: where has chivalry gone? Ended, through.

The left hates meaning, hierarchy and roots.

They're also very social as well: If the group agrees they don't really care what the truth is.

Isolated on their side in echo chamber and having no contact with others, they run from discussions.

The leftists are astonishingly lacking in self-reflection, especially with their beliefs being questioned.

Since they refuse to analyze their own beliefs or themselves, it's just like dealing with children.

Women adopt these views for peer acceptance which is more important to them than security.

Women crave peer approval regardless of ideology.

LIBERAL

In courts, a man's facade of strength is weakness, a woman's facade of weakness is her strength.

All the brethren of the poor do hate him...he pursueth them with words, yet they are wanting to him. Prov 19:7

Women will assume the views of anyone who controls the narrative. Wow-- that's not saying much.

Women have divorced from reality based politics.

Glorifying thuggery and misogyny, that's the grammy.

Fake news, garbage journalism, the worst: that's how POTUS sees CNN and others, our national curse.

POTUS is working so hard for us, up until 2 am every night checking and rechecking cuz he's the best.

Teaching children to be rebellious, ridiculous mental patients.

Insanity in Catholic schools of today: "Mother" and "father" you can't say cuz it may hurt somebody.

The 80's: black community was spiffy, gentlemanly, spiritual, aspiring but globalism demeaned em.

It's women who are to blame for this flood of users cuz they're emotional and love foreigners.

Rural voters are a core threat to our democracy. MSNBC

Politicians benefit more from importing grateful democrats after telling us not to have kids.

LIBERAL

Old fashioned men with values, ethics, morals: can they be found, is there anyone in the human pound?

It's hard to be moral, ethical and have restraint. It's easy to be a sleaze/a thief then driven insane.

Ray always wants to do the right thing and for that he's old fashioned, ridiculous or a saint?

Women's wrath: Tenacity creates cruelty if she's a liberal without wisdom or the desire for liberty.

Of course not all women are dumbed but they're too many that are. Break out, get wise, be a star.

We need federal troops now to the sick, disgusting, degenerate cesspool of San Francisco.

Liberals have such great compassion you know, they care so much about the girl killed on skid row.

Where is the outrage from feminists? They're more interested in campus rape that doesn't exist.

California is part of the third world: Bums kill and go free, jurors fixed, streets filled with feces.

Brad drank to adapt to Jolie: all feminists accuse men of "violent rages" cuz that's the narrative.

Middle aged women with fake ethnic clothes and hippy esoteric beliefs say "let em all in, please".

Phony feminists would rather be queens on a sinking ship than stay on course and be legit.

LIBERAL

Many liberal women furious at their conservative (nationalist) husbands--in divorce they try to ruin them.

Liberal female will take the kids/not let him see them, take everything he has or throw in trash bin.

Racist, bigoted, stupid and wrong. That's what liberals called me in my own family (progressive throng).

If one's premise is liberal they make fools of themselves: it contains the punishment within itself.

We can't fit those churches filled with compromise, carnality and crazy liberals (merely social).

A whole generation who can't think. Plus their parents and grandparents, no wonder we stink.

If I couldn't act right (say what they wanted me to say/not say what they didn't) it was bye bye baby.

Unless it's Americana and their history they recapture, the identity of white Americans will be nowhere.

Facebook is a self-affirming illusion cuz your visitors say "you're right"--echo chamber delusion.

Liberal wives destroying nationalist husbands all over the land (so sad) feeling a "right" to be mad.

When the most important laws aren't followed they must add a million trivial ones/nothing's allowed.

Carnal Christianity (signs): It's a matter of pastors compromising on all things, not just that.

LIBERAL

Poor whites living in trailer parks from abusive families are privileged? Must confront this/resist.

So if you deny you have white privilege it's just a further testament to it's existence? Rubbish!

All I can remember is the second grade. Everything after to here was tainted by sick culture/degraded.

I was about seven when I left heaven and went into leaven: that was my public school education.

Chatter and cackling laughter. I don't know how to communicate like that-- either deep talk or not.

If it's hot, cold, mild; if there are extreme events or none, it's all global warming so don't deny it son.

ISIS is dead and stock market's at an all-time high and you liberal idiots still say he's a bad guy?

Silly sickening Barrack: trying to stay relevant with the claque by saying he loves rock and is black.

Course they're sinning they can't think beyond their inferior and insane public school beginnings.

As they mutilate reality they confiscate history and culture too as we're held guilty by feminist shrews.

Give up your core values and you capitulate into extinction and that's exactly what's happening.

Colleges cherry-pick the worst part of our history to brand us racist, not that we went to war to resist.

It's so trendy to bash whites every idiot is doing it and getting sky-high likes.

LIBERAL

Sick liberals think babies should be killed even after birth and for that they should lose their shirts.

Multiculturalism and political correctness is: cultural Marxism.

Short lesson on science and academia: One books changes nomenclature then it changes each year.

Science and academia aren't stable or reliable--they change with the rabble.

Is it charity or brainwashing device? Always ask this of the nice.

There is no "power" in the devil, only enslavement and failure/evil.

Campuses cautiously train freshmen against subtle insults as tolerance for everyday speech plummets.

The only test for intellectuals is if other intellectuals go along with it (join the hypnotized fools).

Microaggressions: What matters is how the comment is perceived--thus anything can be guilty.

Instead of the war (oppression) between Bourgeois and Proletariat it's now race and gender.

The big churches love the "migrant" invasion receiving billions to "take care" of these invaders.

The leader of the modern peace movement Barrack Obama dropped more bombs than any of them.

Modern day racism is exclusively anti-white but that's all ok with the left as they continue this blight.

LIBERAL

You can't even say it's ok to be white.

Truth: racial diversity is a terrible weakness.

Do whites in Appalachia benefit from their skin color? We must banish this racism of the hour.

Racism is a natural God-given defense mechanism to mitigate against toxic invasion. amen.

Racism saved the tribe since the beginning of time, it's how it is and can't be changed by liberal slime.

Even so we're not a racist country but it's extremely magnified by white liberals and politicians.

So what are you doing for anti-white racism? I thought so, you don't understand anything ma'am.

Why have politicians championing diversity escaped to the most white places? Notice this in all cases.

Forced diversity means fewer friends, less trust, less volunteerism but more television.

As you mature you'll become more nationalist because you see it serves your personal interests.

In this new age of diverse progressives it's not important that you be truthful just that you be nice.

The very idea of sending the child-bearing sex into combat is breathtaking and stupefying. Jarad Taylor

Liberals hate you and your family.

LIBERAL

 I cannot forget how you bashed me at family dinners for not going along with feminist slogans.

I cannot forget how you bashed me for white privilege so I ended up in a shack while you were rich.

We love his crudity, his outspokenness raw truthfulness but you snowflakes implode from realness.

Hello, it's been a long time. While I made a mint from conservative rhyme you're still in liberal slime.

Will you love diversity as cool when your child is the only white one in school?

"Diversity is a strength" is a slogan they just state but can never defend.

Black unemployment is the lowest it's ever been in recorded history. Trump

White people love feeling good about themselves by feeling bad about being white. Jarad Taylor

Liberals vs. the right: Nothing makes them feel more virtuous than apologizing for being white.

"White privilege" teaches non-white people to hate us--or mug us to get some of that unearned gratis.

He who controls the past controls the future. George Orwell

Leftist democrats care more about illegal aliens than American citizens,

Women confuse virtue signaling with politics. It's created a mess and made them and us sick.

Trump tells the truth, he's real and raw while Obama glibly lied while handing us a bunch of bull.

LIBERAL

You think you're so smart cuz you chirp the party line but don't know a thing ex-friends of mine.

Who's bringing these people in: the churches and women. They want big gov/open borders, hmmm.

Don't see how men can stand women the way they chime in with mental illness/social hypnotism.

They're so self-righteous in their idiocy: the Dunning-Kruger Effect. Show you're smart: just don't talk.

Haughty broads and their selfies & silly slogans not knowing a thing about what they're talkin

Protesting trivia while ignoring the devastation everywhere, that's the women's march I do declare.

If you're not a phony virtue signaler women will reject you every time--they hate realness sublime.

So what if women reject you, know who you're dealing with. They're liberals steeped in slogans/myths.

Feminists hate real women too so it's not just you. You don't conform to their BS learned in schools.

Real women don't object to these words because they know it first: a liberal feminist is a curse.

I feel so much better since I blocked you babes from Borrego. You're all virtue signalers and the foe.

You think you're all for women but mere globalist pawns. These are anti-female issues you want.

LIBERAL

Women thinking they're tough when they're not. They don't know a thing about survival/can't tie a knot.

Men are nationalists, women are the problem. I'd gladly give up my vote to cut them out, the fallen.

"Open borders", "no human is illegal"--some of the signs of the women's march of the dumb/un-regal.

They want your approval, man. That's why they say this and that wanting a smile/pat on the back.

I can always read a female by her political views. If she's like Joy Behar or Whoopi, Pee-Uuu.

And they get so angry defending their virtue signaling, so self-righteously indignant, loud, boring.

You're afraid to stand up to the witch but this is holding you back with your home stuck in the ditch.

Not your approval, she wants female peers--the female community is a block to genius and seers.

These anti-Trump baby killers don't realize they're serving Satan but we still detest them.

Our problem is the churches and women who wanna let em all in: Pawns of globalists and deep in sin.

The more we let in the smaller pieces of the pie for us but these crazy women can't see this.

Women are a bunch of friggin' virtue signalers thinking that's politics and making the country sick.

Said in truth to the fat, obnoxious and uncouth.

LIBERAL

I feel I'm surrounded by evil. What I write about is what I feel.

Women are to keep the morals of the household--the "keepers of the hearth" it is called.

He brings an evil spirit into the house, she puts up with it--then their home lives degrade, believe it.

The liberal constantly spews whiney crap, perversion and corruption but always as a "nice person".

Whites aren't attacking anybody but are always blamed. Violence comes from the left, untamed.

A female dominated campus culture always talks about healing not learning.

The loving liberals are enemies of you, your family and your people.

Either develop our own country or be ground down to nothing quickly.

Obama knew the brawn of nonwhites would subsume us so insisted on integrated neighborhoods.

Humans are herd animals: prefer to be in the majority. It can't be overcome so this is our tragedy.

Our consideration for others perverts to pathological altruism in spurts.

The competent are taxed to subsidize the proliferation of the incompetent: imagine that.

The law-abiding well-living are taxed so the lawless can be more self-indulgent and less giving.

Listen to the inspiring liberal message: from "we will overcome" to "we will overthrow".

LIBERAL

Liberals are no-good people worshipping themselves in an echo chamber of self-involved duds.

They need red carpet gatherings so they can feel better about being wrong with all their frivolities.

Lowlifes need constant attention and admiration from each other: it's a laugh to those going higher.

"Racism won't end until all the white people are dead". Oprah Winfrey

Women's march: "We have all the black and brown voting as we want, now you guys get in line too."

Magnify "the march" to make it look bigger than it is then lionize it to make it look pure and noble.

It's like day and night: the dark women in spirit supporting abortion and whatever vs. the pro-lifers.

You can predict women's votes--they're vastly democrat and hate their republican husbands.

The democrats take money from men and give it to their ok-women.

The pro-life rally was about God, family and unborn children. Compare that to evil/immature women.

It's not about race it's about good vs. evil written all over your face.

Oprah is part of the state in charge of families--dismantled as they're taught men are enemies.

Oprah's put out there with pretty face and nice smile as she sells us cultural death as the new style.

LIBERAL

God said male and female. The two women kissing each other is perversion and bound to fail.

Nasty defined: filthy, dirty, defiled, profaned.

Unhappy people control other's lives but happy people just wanna be left alone until they die.

The filthy liberal pigs must self-justify any way they can so they get together as mutual fans.

God hates abortion, homosexuality and intoxication to name a few--but repent and you're straight too.

Barry knew everything, but what will the consequences be?

I knew, we all knew, we let it go--but now the jig is up, times up, whew.

Antifa is scum, they're paid. One was paid 20,000 a year to go around and create hell in spades.

Right-wing rallies: neat as a pin, quiet. Liberal rallies: trash everywhere, insanity, chaos/they deny it.

The left is violent and rowdy, the right is poised and happy but eventually we will fight back, buddy.

Donald Trump is bringing us together, the heart of 1776. We will fight back if you continue your tricks.

The new human is without gender/family, just an animal in a collective with government as zookeeper.

People like Barrack and Hillary were just pandering you--must understand, it's all talk of a shrew.

LIBERAL

I demand reparations for all the money stolen for being white.

Whites are gentler and more refined and easily taken advantage of--good nature perverted.

Liberals say between everything there is moral equivalence (except us) and it's getting ridiculous.

Everything they thought was stereotyped, tired and old. Nothing was original, tho' loud and bold.

Liberals are into soy lattes--these are men addicted to estrogen, making them nuts or like women.

The kids: it's all about signaling to each other they're cool cuz they chirp the crap learned in school.

The coasts are liberal and lost--people are expatriating to middle America which is safe and patriotic.

Captive by a false ideology leftists think suppression of truth is justified for the greater good.

Wickedness is mankind's default setting. Christian restraint comes from strength not weakening.

Inclusion means: everyone matters but you.

We don't want our children and grandchildren to become a minority in a country their ancestors built.

Every race has pride and that's ok but if I'm proud of my heritage it's "white supremacy" and not ok?

We don't want white power, privilege/supremacy. All we want is to be left alone in our own country.

LIBERAL

Whites are told to "celebrate diversity" even though it means our dwindling influence as a minority.

Celebrate diversity while your culture is being displaced. That's part of their plan calling you "privileged".

There is no peaceful happy cum-bay-yah multiracial nation anywhere yet they force it on without care.

Made to feel guilty at 16 for white privilege and thus started decades of addiction and bad self image.

The lives of elite whites who have changed policy to let in the whole world are not one bit damaged.

Elite whites unaffected by diversity themselves force it on those who can't escape the bad results.

We don't hate blacks or Mexicans we hate elite whites who force it on those who can't escape em.

It's an escalating displacement as new immigrants take our money and thus there are less births.

It's ok to be prosperous when the others are not. That's the American way: you work, things work out.

California, Chicago, Frisco and other liberal strongholds are poor, corrupt, tyrannical hell holes.

When they see their country slipping thru their fingers, on a deep level they think: no more youngsters.

Subconsciously whites think: why bring kids into a world where they're a hated minority?

LIBERAL

 Whites have a unique form of psychological capitulation, unwilling to defend their group interests.

Those who say the races are equivalent have not been around other races or they're just nuts.

The idea of NO differences between races led to women in the military--the next step in this tragedy.

Acceptance of racial equality opened the door to one absurdity after another, like fat is better

Caring for their own interests most men have the wisdom to know it's best to be nationalists.

The biggest slaveowners were black.

Identity politics is life distraction. Recall before this: enjoying a sunset, first dating, going on vacation.

Third wave feminism is delusional rape culture while never blaming the true vultures doing it for sure.

The democrats are so weak on crime that they will pay a big price in the next elections. Donald Trump

The sick and dying society hears with it's eyes, speaks with it's genitals and thinks with it's feelings.

The happy well society hears with discernment, speaks God's truths and thinks with common sense too.

Put down Trump to deflect from their filthy, despicable and corrupt dealings-- ignore lemmings!

LIBERAL

You may have learned right in the family but the schools made you dense: without moral sense.

Virtue signaling on an accepted view--wow, you're an intellectual, Sue!

I can't forget you loved the smooth and phony Obama and even Hillary a criminal worst in history.

The democrat party was taken over by communists in the 1970's and you love their stinking anomalies?

People like Antifa and liberals: certifiably nuts going way beyond Trump Derangement Syndrome.

Obama lied to us eloquently and constantly and you still love that destroyer creep/it's not funny.

Expect me to forget how you went along and fell into the popular groove, just to be approved?

Expect me to forget how you loved Hillary, and still do? Of all her filthy doings you approved?

Expect me to forget all the white privilege crap--how you bashed and fired me and put them up?

Obama lied to us eloquently Trump tells the truth crudely--I prefer the latter so much better, truly.

You have pushed us too far--even calling for white genocide cuz you know they don't care.

I can't forget how you were so social you neglected your dog or family members needing you hog.

LIBERAL

I cried all the time, couldn't tolerate it. Luckily I moved to a safe place so could try to forget it.

Well I will forgive all this cuz I'm a Christian and I'm supposed to but doesn't mean I need you pal.

I can't forget how you preferred such trivial things while ignoring or bashing my inner richness.

In communism the most serious crime is individualism.

Antifa (the left) is promoting modesty culture (Islam) because they both want the west bought down.

When liberal fools attack conservatives there's always a severe backlash as they fall on their ass.

I'm with Trump--fire em all--until once in awhile you'll find an ace not the common ordinary dense/small.

Admit it you were ridiculous but Jesus erased it.

I don't have time to explain your bad taste.

They paint Trump as toxic masculinity, sexist oppressor, big bad patriarchy.

"Intolerance of ambiguity is the mark of an authoritarian personality": Bull from Theodor Adorno.

Vegans may smoke cigarettes or fight for other people's children's' right to choose their own gender.

Art transcends it all. Find a musician or inventor, they aren't fighting over religion, politics or culture.

LIBERAL

 The weaponized irrational attacks against our president Sarah Sanders handles with acumen.

It's the feminists putting down Sarah Sanders: they don't support women but shame em as losers.

Watch out for anyone demanding you trust em when they haven't proven--a sign of bad or somethin'.

Capitalism would not be possible without the Protestant work ethic.

Leftists: rehearsed and childish answers, prickly but shallow conversations.

Sarah Sanders can handle the fake news handlers cuz she's got kids and knows about finaglers.

Their pictures are of laughing hyenas, like they're have a party but it's all baloney to impress ya.

They travel to Paris to impress their friends but then step over turds/trash over every bend.

Antifa are beta male soy boy cucks using the system's protection to go out and be thugs.

I have only one life and will transmute this to good.

They feel like they're part of the ruling class when they're not--that's how they're ensnared into rot.

Sarah Sanders is only 35 yet she confronts their lies--so they despise and cut her down to size.

Dark stars: Youth emulating drug addled sexual degenerates are switching to better exemplars.

LIBERAL

Kruger-Dunning effect: saying they can do it when they can't.

Biggest lesson in hiring: everyone says they can do it (but few can)--you must be skeptical/intuit man.

God hates unequal weights. You've been favoring things/those God disdains, bringing ill-fame.

The fascist destroyers won't stop with statues, they'll smash everything western into the future.

Destroy statues then rob us of good role models. Instead we get them, idiots who burn it all down.

Statues are reverence for our ancestors and their achievements but the left can't stand that.

Tho' he has delivered on his promises and will do far more, they refuse to give him any credit so far.

They all say they can do it but none can so I'm getting real good at firing and then starting again.

Saying they can when they can't--get away from me I've had enough of that.

They are computer-wise but common sense, reason and logic-dumb.

After Jolie falsely accused him Brad is seeking escape (never wants to see her again) for 100 million.

Anything--he'll pay anything--to get away from the false accuser like we see in all divorce courts.

Political drama can make us sick and sad or relieved and glad. It's too much, I'm gonna take a nap.

LIBERAL

Good is seen as bad and bad good and even the police will protect (and then release) the hood.

They already had a big head and now our coddling makes em ridiculously nervy (want us dead).

All these decades they looked up to us, now they're here and are loving replacing us, full of sass.

The white man is hated in every corner. This will not end well, it's the effect of Dunning-Kruger.

They think they're smarter than they are, even told they're intellectuals, a new breed/gold star.

They're using satanic hand signs (horns) and have no idea what it is or wouldn't care (like porn).

Now you know how to spot em. You know their buzzwords that instantly peg em as scum.

You're the ace taking great delight in spotting and putting creepy conformists in their place.

It's busting through this screen--the resistance to genius in social cultures--giving you sheen.

She slept with every man in town even husbands. We're not supposed to slut-shame just be fans.

Slut- and fat-shaming are necessary to save sick race but they've banned this cuz it's now all-ok.

It's too bad about him, he should love me though I'm fat and if not he's a misogynist sexist rat.

LIBERAL

"I have sex with everyone but I'm a good person" she said--even bragged about it like Blanche did.

Don't argue, don't relate. You're higher, you know their game and their fate.

The effects of groups on consciousness: How fascinating as we learn that more is actually less.

It is catastrophic to be framed by people. Frame yourself or let God, simple.

No use being angry at em just see em as little children needing pablum so start today, tell em.

When they start up, don't go down that rabbit hole with them. Don't object or debate cuz you know em.

Viewing self against the ground of "them" you fall short but without em it perfectly hits the mark.

The result of being framed by them is shame or guilt but framed by God is infinity and depth.

You're absolutely inspired, what do you have to feel guilty about? That's from them, a black cloud.

Reason for fires in their words for y'all: California wants compact development to reduce sprawl.

California wants stack-housing to reduce sprawl and they also won't allow rural living for y'all.

The desktop Manual fits perfectly historically. It is hyper-synchronicity for this generation, truly.

LIBERAL

 We all know a good female role model. Just emulate her not the modern day rabble (they are awful).

Men, stop apologizing. It's pathetic you've been pushed this far but just repent and be uncompromising.

Speak for the heartbreak of your generation--like unconscious collective archetypes of man.

To get concealed carry, know how to shoot a pistol at short range and random killings are changed.

Just one person with concealed carry coulda saved twenty.

Scumbags like him are the reason for our 2nd amendment.

California burn plan will spread nationwide. They want us in city ghettos and not on the land.

The evil side of humanity plugging into high tech systems.

Wanna move em to the cities--that's why they're burning out Californians (even horses) on purpose.

Debauched and dirty 18th century England: the reaction *against* all that was the Puritans.

Are you the woman who publicly puts down her own father and her Savior?

What was so fascistic about it was how you enjoyed excluding me and I will never forget that.

Didn't wanna let me in cuz they'd have to change everything since I'm opposed to sinning.

It's hyper-synchronicity--it fits in history. You know what's happening, it's beyond evil thinking.

LIBERAL

Which is worse: Hollywood or it's emulators? What about kin/friends acting like asinine imitators?

If they hate Trump or use buzzwords like "global warming" or like concepts, heed my warning.

Tho' they've done nothing, they deserve fame and fortune. That's the progressives but they're done.

Rule 1: Don't argue with em. Rule 2: Don't even think of em.

There's no way I'd ever grace their dumb liberal shows and argue with those who don't know.

And having to deal with *that*–are you kidding me? In your *home*?

"Likes" is no barometer of your value so get offa that thing

It's a progressive disease like anything else, but our constitution gives us freedom to do this.

Antifa is an adolescent group of idiots fighting with knives and bricks.

Remember how sick you were around em? Liberal climate does that so best to release em.

Sodomism means Homosexual supremacy.

HaHa a big fat cow preening on the red carpet. Isn't she marvelous this know nothing and a mess.

Don't start me on lesbians in the area--the most brazen and pugnacious group in America.

They've gotta hammer it in they're right--cuz inside they know they're wrong, saying bigots be gone.

LIBERAL

By your attraction to the fake you've ruled out association with a most golden opportunity to take.

It's sickening: unnatural parings or anything else preposterous/erring, a depthless evil thing.

If they hate Trump, take joy! Now you know who to leave out or who will surely disappoint.

If someone loves Hillary, laugh it off. Back off, forget em: peanut galleries who mock and scoff.

I know you from your likes and will use that as a barometer to rid myself of you drippy hangers: yikes.

Just the fact you like that/think you're on the red carpet yet a TV addict but forget you, I fixed it.

Sickening isn't it, they could think like that? But that's the human tribe vs. God's men, His beloveds.

Since whole cultures go down together we must study social hypnotism the most--and it's here.

Women make fools of selves/show no power saying things like "my colleague, a nobel prize winner"...

Stand up/defend middle America not the leftist coasts, standing for wrong until they're toast.

Monsters on red carpet: jewels in a pig's snout.

They take you down cuz you are right and they are wrong.

We're sick of coastal liberals making decisions for us, the real.

LIBERAL

I earned my independence from years of seeing what happens when you lose it.

How could you let these women take over like this? Nothing so much proves liberalism is false.

That's all there is out there: interconnecting realities fused together in a big hypnotic scare.

They are scary to clear minds: so dense, so heartless, so out of touch thinking they know much.

The culture-stealers have gone so far as to say we should feel proud for obesity or being slutty.

Things that would have meant a looney bin are now front and center as superior while we be enablin'

Canadians have had enough of Trudeau's leftwing ideology and he'll be gone to forestall a tragedy.

Men: you've gotta stop apologizing. Although so endearing it is all from social engineering.

Men you're gotta stop listening to crazy women or like Merkel a whole continent will fall to vermin.

Men: I know you want peace at any price, tranquility and sex so you tolerate feminist dogma, a hex

Copying a man's world of money wheeling/dealing, women are easily bought off—loyalty's not thought of.

What a great pleasure to live in this era where I can find out things 20 hours a day then tell ya.

LIBERAL

Don't call it "new age" call it liberalism cuz conservatives restore the old paths for success/optimism.

America needs to be aligned with a Christian nation reforming itself: Russia.

It's so disgusting the coastal liberals' superficial sheen while inside, filthy things they believe in.

What an embarrassment these loser liberals about to fall. They aren't ready/don't know guns at all.

Putin sees Barrack and Hillary clearly and loves Trump. This man is our ally not our enemy hon'

As Obama/Clinton/Podesta go down people will see how it's evil Soros' globalist machinations.

Obama bought $65,000 hotdogs (boys) but you think Trump is bad (how liberal thinking disappoints).

They're as dumb as rocks but humans spout slogans by rote: no true smarts but it blocks ya know.

Coastal liberals see themselves as intellectuals. Can you believe that? We'll soon see you fools.

It is race discrimination to not want to hire criminals?

Without God they'll believe anything--any kooky rubbish demons think of.

Not Christian if they "love Jesus" the man/prophet but don't see Him as exclusive/they can't do that.

Americans are sinners too but somewhere still inside is the Christian work ethic that built this country.

LIBERAL

Of course climate change exists but it's not man-made or to pay them carbon taxes.

It used to be the churches were for charity now government is as the churches become a rarity.

See the signs, nip it in the bud: that's a true leader like Trump.

They object to your correction then make the same darn mistake again.

It's horror dealing with zombies in charge of your nice life and things.

Due to the Dunning-Kruger effect of dummies thinking they're smart, if you correct them they object.

Computer warning: Don't waste time cuz you can get way out in left field, tangentialized.

In a chaotic era like ours people slip into weird archetypes and templates yet they can't see it.

Hillary does not love women if she's still married to a sexual predator and convicted rapist, vermin.

What if it were a child chained like that? I know it's a dog but they both have feelings/are sentient.

I used to be a feminist, even taught women's studies. I'm the opposite now after decades of curses.

They're for women--but love Hillary who's still married to a serial, convicted rapist/sadist.

He bit the victim's lip until it bled and that got her into bed but feminists love the Clintons instead.

LIBERAL

It goes underground: she's happier but soon subconscious wisdom sets in and she's snippier.

What accounts for the hysterical female outburst? Sick cycles of denial vs. love, deceit vs. trust.

Weaker he is the more stripes come out cuz self-restraint takes strength and he's dropped out.

No psychiatrist can sort it out where lies and love co-exist. If he's in denial he's a liar and you're pist.

Your minimizing of sin (because it's prevalent) is so telling, but I'll forget it.

A womanizer's rehab: learning not to do it in front of her.

Eminem made a fool of himself at SNL--see what happens when you come against Trump the marvel?

I am sorry the tattoo will blur with age and look even dirtier. But you still must face it's not prettier.

Who are you to mark up the body God gave you. It's ugly, the bible says it's what the heathen do.

Does the wife ever think he's exhibiting for the nurses? No, it's always just an accident not sex curses.

Take hold of shield and buckler, and stand up for my help! Psalms 35: 2

For a couple hours I was terrified of his black and evil powers but I won't forget God will shower.

A zebra can't change it's stripes. He is what he is, there are bad seeds who are unsalvageable I guess.

LIBERAL

What destroys marriages: sin. What repairs/makes good ones: repentance, starting all over again.

Bashing men when they're the ones who can protect them. Becoming less attractive, too easy giving in.

Becoming less attractive because he should love you anyway, but hey that's not the way to be lady.

If you don't be sweet lil' ladies, you'll be driven crazy or killed and you created the tragedy.

Ultimately all you can do is forgive then start again to live.

Love and abandon reality. Give that all up and then really see the sick relationship, a tragedy.

That devil is so dominating and peremptory too, I feel great peace every time I bid him adieu.

Share everything and make you feel guilty if you don't. It's all bull we're independent/this ain't God.

It's not just a white nationalist thing. Different but equal as everyone is happiest when separated.

Camille Paglia (famous feminist) is all for abortions, a heartless sadist or an intellectual, sis?

People cannot be equalized upwards so it means downwards, the lowest common denominator.

The hoax of black victimization and those who enable it. Colin Flaherty

Makes me sick you thinking I should accept that.

LIBERAL

They wanna makes us in *their* image but then leave cuz it's a pig sty.

Equal but different/separate: otherwise it's conflict--like how you treat dogs-- and we're sick of it.

The only cure for non-assimilation is a fifty year ban on immigration.

Ban newcomers and there is eventual assimilation of the others, or it's just more enclaves/no-goers.

Diversity is not only not our strength but completely destroys community cohesion. Robert Putnam

In London, knife crime is up 34% and 13,000 stabbings from invadees.

Christian children taken to Muslim foster homes.

Christianity faltered and was replaced by religion of equality (modernity) both political and economic.

Don't give me your false Christianity. We live in an age of prevalent pedophilia and it's all ok with ya?

Since a filthy sin is common we're supposed to accept it? Believe it or not, many pastors ignore it.

To so-called "pastors": Stop calling filthy sins of Satan a "sickness" then begin to heal as Christians.

Left is trying to sexualize children so they're conditioned to it. Like justifying pedophiles, think about it.

He was always into pornography calling it "German movies".

LIBERAL

 **Pastors make it worse by condemning the scorned wife for her "hate" and saying he's just "sick".**

Jesus was a real man taking on the temple of cheats. He didn't justify, comply or accept defeat.

The only freedom is freedom from illusion. Stefan Molyneux

You sound like the pope the way you justify this filth. What has happened to Christians/moral health?

Touching a child is as bad as penetration when it comes to tragic lifelong effects on the victim.

Saudis letting em date now but everything is above board not casual sex right away like here.

Immigration laws should benefit the people in the country, not those outside of it obviously.

If your enemy has a sword, get a bigger one. Christianity is not about being a wimp and laying down.

As smart as Milo is, he's indecent. Decency is our matrix, barometer and litmus test, amen.

Demographics is destiny but questioning government makes us a conspiracy theory.

People died so how dare you question the official story!

I'm not going to argue with some lawyer, just take the money you shyster-- profession of poor character.

"Racism" is here defined: You care about your own race and you know that all races are different.

LIBERAL

We're strong but also most fragile. We break, we go under but given the right fodder we go higher.

How much of the outsider can you tolerate? That is the breaking point.

Whites have been told they don't even exist, why protect what is theirs?

Women have played a major role in the migrant crisis in Europe--more xenophilic and emotional.

White self-interest is not racism: accepting all groups have interests fosters mutual understanding.

EcoScience final assault: depopulate the planet by confusing gender and putting chemicals in food/water.

Blacks were highminded and creative: look at Soul Train! Then MTV made em thugs/into drugs.

This was all subversion thru entertainment and we were all part of it--now thugs top the grammy list!

Bad boys and bad girls are sick freaks but actually have very high self-esteem, billionaires it seems.

I was unequally yoked to an ex-Obama intern posing as a virtual assistant, can you believe that?

They can sexualize infants--Kinsey proved that in the sixties. A longterm plan, Lord come please.

Making kids non-gender is part of a UN plan to depopulate the planet, for decades we've known it.

Is it a boy or a girl? Let the state and it's programming decide, not you.

LIBERAL

America has become coarse, pornographic, anti-man--it all goes together cuz women hold the line.

Disney caught in shocking sexualization of babies, not even infants, and you love liberals/Hillary?

Don't forget how brilliant these founders were, kept us free all that time. But now there is unholy swine.

Women are largely shallow/can't see what they're doing to me, you, the whole world/no more free.

They think they're being nice and loving and are so blind they can't see the destructive people-flooding.

Virtue-signaling and liberalism is so obviously a mental illness and I don't see how we can last.

Women are rabid sloganizers but to them peer acceptance is more important than *what* ideas.

Women: they got us into this mess and are still getting us into it--will real men come forward, please?

Just the fact peer approval is more important than *what* ideas show's where women are at, geez

The sexualization of babies is truly the next level of depravity from Disney.

Their first word is not "mama" or "papa" but "smash the patriarchy".

Watch out for leaks to the street. Whether gossip-called-concern or social manipulators do speak.

It wasn't "Sheila" it's that most women are like Sheila and the morals she lacked.

LIBERAL

No one wants to hear about the huge differences between genders/races--to liberals they're all aces.

Boys not doing well in school, males seen as bad, men live shorter lives, wives snipe, mock, despise.

Son, what must you do to be a man? "I have no clue, no guidelines, no rules, masters nor scripts".

Be ladies & gentlemen not groveling supine minions.

The dumb tend to be social--the smart don't have time, finding it silly cuz they've got goals.

God said we'd be despised, put aside, walked on by, framed by those who lied, on the wrong side.

The dumber they are the more social. I always thought so, I'd so prefer to be creative all alone.

The dumb are much more social cuz what else do they have but yak-yak-yak or they'd go mad.

There's only two ways to fix things in life: the club (force) or your words. Stefan Molyneux

Lady found the compromised church boring and social and the gentleman said he'd never again go.

And to think we hated all that syrupy sentimentality, after going thru this we want it all back, truly.

I have no children--will leave my fortune to saving dogs from Asian dog-meat operations.

LIBERAL

When you're expected to socialize and everyone wears a disguise/spouts lies, impossible guys.

You believe that crap cuz that's what you learned in school. Not your thoughts--it's a plan, subliminal.

Sorry I can't be interrupted. I can't let you determine my day and this lesson I learned the hard way.

Full of bitterness and captive to sin.

It took years to recover from a feminist tyrant over me and when I saw her later she was an old lady.

Ku Klux Klan mentality on the left is what we have today. They own it all including what we say.

Bedlam's occurring in CA cities. They've got the green light now, they can do anything and stay free.

Sanctuary cities are smugglers and criminal aliens best friend.

Where is great compassion of liberals in Frisco? There isn't any--liberalism is just a front ya know.

Life/death of a sea lion is worth more than a white woman in Frisco today: year in jail and big fine, ok?

Tried by a jury of his peers--you mean felons and illegal aliens? Death is near for many Californians.

Liberal newspapers like L.A. Times didn't even report on this. Shocking as lemmings approach the abyss.

Matt Lauer and friends are fake news gatekeepers of lies, distracting you with foolish disguise.

LIBERAL

Why do women support/condone criminals? Same reason they love bad boys tho' it's subliminal.

I'm done with bad boys, there's no attraction there. I like decency in a man and it's so darn rare.

Politics is downstream from culture (coarse, pornographic, anti-man) so we've lost protection.

We love Trump's unpresidentialness.

Women were ok and splendid when sweet lil' ladies but now they're the worst: debauched and shady.

Do not visit San Francisco, see? Cuz if you're mugged, robbed or shot the killer will go free.

Brad Pitt drank cuz he left his first wife. You ensnared him sexually then he felt guilt, shame, strife.

A woman meets another woman, sizes her up and puts her in her place. All thru history that is the case.

Democrats love Lena Dunham who said she wanted to carry a baby so she could abort for "solidarity".

Those who support sanctuary cities are to blame for the death of Kate Steinle. Sean Hannity

Lena Dunham's idea of feminism was to steal car keys and not give a bleep what her father thinks.

As a boomer who cut corners it was a shock as he went by-the-book on everything, but it took.

They made us hate America and some even changed their names. It was a set-up: we were framed.

LIBERAL

World's worse dictatorships always had an image of benevolence followed by death and hardship.

They made us think nothing of illicit sex but after restoring the old paths we see them as the best.

Don't let em go out unchaperoned. You can't trust anyone and it would be better to be alone.

Don't let your girls out with boys or groups, cuz if they insist on chastity they'll be called fools--true?

It takes rare strength at 16 to go against group's thinking so I'd chaperone and be called crazy.

Satan (and his people) are jealous of God (and His people) so we gotta get hep, fence up, be real.

They read whatever agrees with them then think "everything is fine" when it isn't, they could die.

A self-righteous hack politicizing a tragic death.

Ego blinds so it's easy to use events to grandstand but I'd use restraint to save embarrassment.

She's a self-righteous hack politicizing a tragic death--that's what she was grandstanding like that.

Elites aren't being pushed out of neighborhoods by immigrants so they have "blissful ignorance.".

Having fled from foreigners to do the job I found the Americans were lazy, sleepy, inattentive slobs.

LIBERAL

When you finally find one you can work with (energy), treat him like gold cuz the rest is lunacy.

When you finally find one reliable after going thru the dregs you feel you've won the lottery, it's sick.

Women encouraged to lie about him, do him in, make him pay/suffer, take away his children (vindication).

Sarah Sanders is taking down the press every day like a boss.

We can keep our farms--no estate tax for farmers! For America, Donald Trump is the savior.

As things fail like in California, people fall more into sin I tell ya--then divorces rise in America.

Tho' they do it all wrong still they may hang on but you must fire, avoid, block, take a rest, sing a song.

Your worst enemies will encourage you to do wrong--those "friends" from the liberal throng.

Ben Afflect the liberal pest had ancestors who were slaveowners.

A crazy liberal woman with way too much power. Women are the reason for the mess we're in, wow.

Why so much perversion and sex harassment? Cuza women acting like that, an embarrassment.

Chinese owns California and that's why the fires. They have it planned but it's just business of liars.

You go to California to get poor and you leave to get rich.

LIBERAL

Liberals are syrupy fake nice but wait a minute you'll see their vice.

The ugly, old, washed out Barrack staying relevant with this silly dumbed youth base: "I love rock".

So reckless with my money but so stingy with his own. In those cases it's better being alone.

Men arrested in hospitals for exposing themselves to nurses--they're falling into sick sex curses.

Globalists call liberty movement a fake, fraud, won't deliver but it's the third world in culture wars.

Tyrants and parasites: The left aborts more than half of black children and sexualizes kids too.

Hospital flash: surrounded by young flesh pedophiles can't resist since hospital gowns = easy access.

It's the spirit inside doing the flashing (exhibiting). It's natural for it to do these things.

Martin Luther King is now bad (removed) since he didn't mention LBGTQ tho' it didn't exist then.

Obamacare is legislation by laxative. Greg Gutfeld

Cultural Marxism was the translation from the have/have nots to the oppressors and the oppressed.

"Haves vs. have-nots" didn't work in America so Marxists switched to "racism" during Obama.

LIBERAL

The secret of their influence: the liberal intelligencia pay no price for being wrong (think of that).

If there's a price for being wrong they'd have to think about it, change their ways or be eliminated--not.

Conservatives aren't flawed, they're pragmatic.

The accusation of racism has made small towns devoid of any meaning. Douglas Murray

Intellectuals give people handicapped by poverty a further handicap of victimhood, a real tragedy.

Hollywood dames dress in black but it was liberal buddies doing the groping and this will come back.

The liberal phonies dressed in black can't win cuz it's a setup job--another empty try--but we have God.

The defunct pope lets bare-breasted women feed in sanctuary but it's all ok don't you think, hehe.

Liberals: Do you know what open borders does to dogs? Do you ever think of that, let alone God?

Our dear Trump is getting more audacious and sure of himself every day and I'm so proud, say Hurray!

Whenever he talks of all the starving children in the world you know he's a liberal cuz we can't help that.

Every democrat in congress voted against tax cuts for the American farmer--can they get any meaner?

LIBERAL

Farm country is God's country. Donald Trump

If the democrats had their way they'd reinstate every regulation that's killing us vs. the POTUS.

Not a word about Islamacists killing females--she backs these oppressors but attacks American males.

America's the best place for women but she grandstands so you won't see what a witch she is, man!

If you see em on TV watch their hands by which they always pay homage to the devil's fans.

Why are our American men homeless? Because they can't trade lodging for sex. Stefan Molyneux

Women: It's not that all men are bad but that you chose the wrong man.

On the right, government exists to keep your freedoms but on the left it exists to buy your vote.

We love watching Di Nero do himself in. We love it when you "intellectuals" act like 13-year olds.

The star's $400 shirt read "poverty is sexist".

Swollen corrupt satanic Hollywood.

Queen sees through Meghan, a liberal leftist snowflake who hates Trump and everything decent.

How is she indecent? She wants open borders so we're raped/robbed, effecting our descendants.

Liberals are against Iranian protests by wonderful smart people held down for decades--aren't libs great.

LIBERAL

 All they care about is mean tweets and misgendering people, not about the present widespread evil.

Left says we must punish whites for the past. It's due compensation tho' they're innocent/miscast.

Just cuz it's a trendy topic doesn't make it right. Just cuz it's common doesn't make it legitimized.

Whenever someone says "I'm not trying to screw you" you know he's trying to screw you.

Who's doing all the groping? It's liberals loved by millennials tho' they protest it's all men, what fools.

So sorry to cut into your social life with the other hags on the red carpet bragging like they've made it.

Whoopi says Trump is the Taliban cuz he won't pay for her contraceptives: how ridiculous.

Sadiq Khan has the tranny toilets running but couldn't care less about acid attacks or stabbings.

Gay clubs are fast tracks into homo lifestyle and cruising with adults the vile in this trendy sin in style.

Bad men exist, bad women exist. That doesn't mean all men are bad except to the feminist.

Has embracing left wing politics been bad for the church? Membership collapsed, left em in a lurch.

We need to be re-horrified by homosexuality. Linda Harvey

All through human history homosexuality explodes right before destruction as it brings it on.

LIBERAL

What I saw all around was an emboldened lowlife criminal class dominating small California towns.

California a democrat sanctuary state reflected in debauchery, disrespect, homelessness and trash.

Everything starts in California which I escaped. Hopeless, homeless, trashed, dreams dashed.

In one desert town a gang of teen thugs took over and the cops wouldn't do a thing to these jokers.

Californians are satiated, coerced and sedated into accepting a lower and lower third world state.

"Non-violent" crimes in California: Holding an elderly hostage or raping while drunk--that's just a few bud.

California is a sanctuary state, meaning: it harbors criminals.

Outa California for two years and I'm still edgy, looking over my shoulder--no way to live when older.

California is a shithole too Donald.

In California I was put down, regulated and edgy but here I've got a salon, known for my abilities.

Inner-city criminals spreading out thru small towns who are not equipped to handle this behavior.

As small towns fall hostage to ne're-do-wells there are no repercussions except going to hell.

The naughty boys at fake news love saying "shit hole" all day--360 times, ok?

LIBERAL

Breaking thru delusion is hard with a child being taught--it's the same with all the lies they bought.

Ethno-Nationalism is shared heritage, language, faith, and ethnic ancestry vs. destruction/tyranny.

To solve race problems we can't just chant slogans which are coo coo and wrong.

Your politicians are putting a bunch of dumbass, entitled, evil or illiterate people over you: watch.

That's why they cry, rant and rave. They bought the lies from school starting with the first grade.

While we're all sinners God has put in us a holy hatred for it in all it's forms and thus we're winners.

They attack Christians cuz they don't get angry--until they do.   Stefan Molyneux

Libs said they'd leave if Trump wins so why not move to Haiti, friends?

Little children at CNN love saying a dirty word on TV and getting away with it but we see thru them.

So the little boys got to say the word "shit" all day and pin it on the president, what a trip.

The liberals care so much about Haiti but not the millions raised for it then stolen by Hillary?

Even tho' they say sh*t 10X a day they blow this up instead of the *real* issues which require study.

LIBERAL

I read between the lines, i see tell tale signs. Women are more intuitive than men at all times.

He'd like to shove it onto you as a paranoid psychotic cuz you see the light.

Look at what he's already done, not how he seems--his false image/facade--to stay on the beam.

People are just evil but it's covered over so it doesn't seem real. Track record, that's how you tell.

Wickedness is man's default setting. You gotta be strong to restrain.

You abandoned yourselves to soft prodigal living and to the pleasures of self-indulgence. James 1:5

You have fattened your hearts in a day of slaughter. James 1:5

Whites are bad when they leave (white flight) and bad when they come back (gentrification of blacks).

Arrogance of narcissistic criminals brings them down. Boldness brings success, then the mess.

Fake victim hoaxes mean instant fame and tremendous sympathy for the instigator who is lying.

Like a dog to his vomit he went right back to it: that's the sensual devil as the bible describes it.

They call Trump "crude" cuz he doesn't have a shiny veneer as we're oh so eloquently screwed.

Due to rampant pornography and pedophilia the barbarians line up on the periphery I'll betcha.

LIBERAL

Libs steeped in ridiculous egalitarian notions will switch when pilloried for speaking obvious truths.

It's 40 X more likely for a black to assault whites than the other way around, yet they're told to fight.

"Freedom Acts" etc. are always the opposite: If they incarcerate you they "free everyone else".

They get us all worked up for justice then nothing happens--it all fizzles out. Will they ever arrest the cabal?

He's articulate in left wing ideology but if he loses swings to bad language and attacking the winner.

Never argue with idiots. They will drag you down to their level and beat you with experience. Mark Twain

Eminem sobbing and crying: "It should have been Hillary...wha wha wha wha".

Eminem calls Trump a "f**king turd" because turds prefer turds.

To all you sister wives: I can't even stand to share my man's mind.

The last thing I need is false Christian/liberal female trivializing this or telling me to accept it.

To the woman on facebook wearing the thong: get a life, write a book, sing a song.

They are the "spirit of right and good" and everything else must "bow to their presence".

You act like you need the approval of your silly generation--can't you broaden?

LIBERAL

 The evil are out there deceiving playing the victim role so you believe em and into hell following them.

Do not fall for it: these wicked women and their empty sayings.

Our country was hijacked by fools and traitors destroying our culture.

Scientific revolutions take place one funeral after another. Anonymous

These are no-good people for the things they believe in, evil. Who'd wanna listen with no appeal?

And what of the men involved with feminist slime: weak and pathetic girlie men not worth a dime.

Everyone suffers with divorce. The men horribly, kids, pets! All due to this globalist plan, a curse.

Blacks like Oprah/Obama talk like preachers to emotionalize and brainwash you to be controlled.

Smart blacks stand out and don't like em any better than we do so when hearing the facts: whew.

Who has time to worry about ISIS terrorists when gender pronouns are being disrespected?

Having been taught debauchery and acting on it, seared consciences just can't accept God.

To broadcast his virtue signaling of tolerance while at the expense of competence was the worst.

You can take Oprah outa the ghetto but not the ghetto outa Oprah. --Oprah's mother.

LIBERAL

He watches pornography out of "curiosity" or "study" he says--what a load of bull from scuzz.

He sits there and lies to my face. The mark of mental health is to finally see it as a useless disgrace.

Ha Ha You thinking it's all-ok when it's not. Always pushing envelope making fools of yourselves.

When it's your power/money you share it with me. When it's mine I have a right to be stingy/miserly.

When it's my money I'm to share it with you. When it's yours I'd do well to get a dollar or two.

We never throw the first punch but when you do it, calling us names, we will retort or even insult.

Investigations or political set-ups? Why waste our time unless they're locked up? Do it now, man up.

Always saying he's a man of God but running to sin the first chance he got/the lies you bought.

The divorcee said "his interest in other women's breasts was inveterate and I guess he couldn't help it".

Since they normalized, legitimized and superiorized homosexuality many men go "fishing".

Always talking about "detachment" and "calm" yet going crazy over the smallest of things: bomb.

Read the bible many times but still a nasty Pharisee/grime.

GLOBAL

Satanic doctrine: out of chaos comes order.

Don't we have a right to remain a majority in our own country established by our ancestry?

Diversity is just as totalitarian as Stalin, a completely new concept of designed societies failin'

Your race is your nation and your nation is your family--but now that's all gone, it cannot be.

Whites have built successful societies and that's why non-whites want to come.

Being suddenly surrounded by strangers is one type of God's wrath.

Displacement of populations is no different from armed invasion.

Those rich white liberals who can afford to sequester themselves from chaos bring em in.

Of course you want what is mine, and invite your whole family in for more pieces of the pie.

Oh, the poor immigrants--and not one word about what's happening to us citizens being crushed.

Tho' they say it's swell diversity is hell and NO one likes being under it's spell.

A small clique managing the decline of Europe and letting her fall. It's so sad, horrible and unbelievable.

GLOBAL

There is a suicidal double standard for whites to accept the replacement of their own people.

Is it so wrong for us to resist being reduced to a hated minority thru uncontrolled immigration?

The more different we are the less we agree. People prefer to hang with their own or it's catastrophe.

"Diversity consulting" is a ten billion dollar a year industry and that's just the beginning of this fallacy.

If it's so wonderful why spend 10 billion a year to manage it? Cuz it's torture and we don't want it.

The generally good things in life do not require "consulting" they just are while we are enjoying it.

This poisonous ideology has defanged and neutered us into spineless cuckolds. Jarad Taylor

Why is it wrong for whites to wish to remain a majority in their own country? As usual, there is no reply.

We do not want parallel societies, population exchanges or the replacement of Christian civilization.

Mass migration is masquerading as humanitarian cause but it's true nature is occupation of territory.

The globalists keep everyone down, Trump wants to empower everybody in nation and town.

Men are nationalists, God love em. Women vote big government and open borders--fools, all of em.

GLOBAL

Globalist's parasitic behavior is making people poor to control them--that's it's *one* symptom.

The liberals show insanity, equating normal immigration laws with white racism and bigotry.

It's surrealistic the passage of time when such a decent and outstanding clan is replaced by slime.

Replace the kindest, most humane and decent civilization with the most barbaric, cruel, authoritarian.

Why are whites so exploitable when no other race does anything but look out for their own?

Western men gave women freedom, now western women choose Islam to take it away from them.

The major race science claim: There is more difference between groups than within them.

Stop calling them "dreamers" like they're little kids with Ph.D.s. Many on the dole/adults/sleaze.

Race realism is based on biological fact not social construct making life sad.

With the sanctuary cities clogged to the brink it's a matter of public safety not "white supremacy".

A quarter of a billion people want to see the western world suffer. Two separate worlds, need a buffer.

Liberal Europe hates itself too--despite beauty/good food--because guilty cultures submit to fools.

GLOBAL

Western values: democracy, human rights, freedom of expression/worship, secular government.

These values of liberty are superior, but liberals say "it's all the same", period.

It's the democrats who are globalist holding us hostage saying we must keep the border open: pigs!

Nationalism is the wave of the future while multiculturalism has been a disaster.

People want to determine their own destiny in a homogeneous community not forced diversity.

Due to diversity we've lost control of our future, children's education, survival and very destiny.

Why should whites be the only ones happy to be displaced by others? Cultural diversity only smothers.

There's nothing wrong with wanting your grandchildren to resemble their grandparents not aliens.

The lust for egalitarianism is a smash them/silence them sentiment as whites go into extinction.

Whites have the greatest power of abstract reasoning and imagination yet they give in and cower.

White abstraction gives them the ability to ignore reality and so what is good becomes their tragedy.

People happily self-segregate to be with their own, expressing the natural tribalism of humans.

Throw Merkel out and put her in jail.

GLOBAL

Progressives are ok with us getting killed because open borders gives them political power.

Race realism: When the lower IQs don't do as well they blame the higher in a screaming college yell.

More diversity = less trust.

Whites will always find a way to insulate from the brute strangeness or religious weirdness.

Affluent liberals say how great diversity is but they can escape while the poor accept their fate.

Nationalism vs. globalism is between the Heavenly Father and the workings of darkness is high places.

Women are terrible voters cuz they love big government and open borders.

Oprah Winfrey is a top globalist and eugenicist who pushes a one world religion brainwashing children.

Oprah's a race controller in the Rockefeller cult to depopulate blacks all over especially in Africa.

Oprah's main agenda was to disconnect us from all religion and join the Gaia church of globalism.

Oprah is the heart of the Bill and Melinda Gates Foundation, getting rid of husbands/having abortions.

Oprah: the black face of black depopulation and abortion.

We complain of poverty, disease and crime but bring in the poor, diseased and criminals--how divine.

GLOBAL

The herd of elephants in the front yard is mass migration. Ralph Peters

They are more afraid of traditional Americans than illegal immigrants, terrorists, ISIS or gangs.

Stockholm Syndrome is more real than we know. Gang rapes: the Swedes won't help em now.

When your own group won't protect you it's horrifying to humans, like favoring Muslim men.

It is better not to govern than to govern badly. "Merkel, resign" they are saying in Germany.

Merkel's demise: a self-inflicted wound after inviting a million Syrians into her country.

Thanks to Merkel, Germany's swung to far right--something inconceivable before this blight.

You're just gonna have to march in there and arrest her. Save Germany from Merkel mass murder.

If you wanna dress like that in useless material and flowing nuisance go ahead, it's so inefficient.

They're going into it for fashion--just like women always. They know nothing about it, dangerous.

It's the IN thing to do. Only problem is a serpent's about to strike you.

It's the mosques, the styles, the music--I loved Arabian sounds too but later had a different view.

They look like blistering hot costumes. Half monk, half beekeeper outfits.

GLOBAL

If people hate it when their neighborhood changes how can we expect the whole nation to love it?

Diversity wisdom: You can maintain the same country by swapping out a different population.

It's a biological fact that racial differences go way beyond mere skin color and it's infinite sir.

"Race is an illusion" except when granting preference to non-whites son.

Diversity: Insofar as you are enriched I am impoverished so of course you love this.

It's not that we don't care but we put our own first, the most natural thing when not under a curse.

Do you remember the promises he made to you--to restore our way of life so eroded by liberal fools?

The globalists are using Islam as a battering ram to make the Christian west truckle and that's all.

You must suspect--even hate--anyone for open borders. These people are your murderers/torturers.

Kids are the same way--invite people to your home. Social cultures think nothing of invasion, dumb.

It's no small thing inviting people to your home. The mere contact, you're kicked off your throne.

For their short-term gain they're allowing this invasion of belligerents aiming to supplant us/kill us.

GLOBAL

Our dealing with globalist unelected bureaucrats is a form of ritual humiliation. Nigel Firage

Women caused the problem cuz they love big government and open borders (makes me shudder).

Trudeau's policies towards Iran reflect his love of authoritarians.

They'll "progress" us into globalist tyranny, a dark cloud for you and me, and these are friends? I see

Now let me get this straight: you left your dogs, cats and happy comfy home to travel to--Paris?

Teaching "cultural awareness" is preparing them for the worst shock of their lifetime, what a mess.

As a hypersensititive I always knew I should not travel unless I wanted mental illness from the evil.

Hah: They were taught that the rudest city on earth was one of greatest romance, beauty and mirth.

Don't travel unless you want to see sickening evil, like how they treat cats and dogs for example.

How can I trust if you travel to countries where these evils are taking place and you can tolerate?

When the idea they have of the country meets the reality of what they discover, it provokes a crisis.

Ok, I get this: avoid crisis of meeting other reality. Stay in a bubble and enjoy each day happily.

Puritanism sprang up against debauched 18th c. England--it's happening here, stay around.

GLOBAL

My polite and restrained culture then suddenly be confronted like this? Frightening and alarming

Since traveling is sensual, nothing prepares your for the assault of scents, sights, sounds on arrival.

Culture shock may trigger previously undetected (latent) mental disorders and quirks: shock, curse.

Suddenly, genetically determined "quirks" roll out with stress. In happy peace, they didn't exist.

Vitriol: Stark contrast in cultures' sense of politeness, social graces and communication in general.

Sure things happen here but not so much on the surface unless it's NYC or California of course.

A general basis of decency veils discrepancy so we don't have to witness it and that's Americana.

I was ready for the embassy with the other shaking, disillusioned, hallucinating malcontents.

Female anorexia begins with culture shock in college. It's mental illness after a safe/orderly house.

Girl leaves decent orderly home for college and loses mind, binges or self-starves from the chaos.

Culture shock brings depression, especially since no reality testing about what is best/efficient.

They keep going home--to escape chaos and return to order which is best and evokes the creative.

GLOBAL

Many can compartmentalize, so to see the Eiffel Tower they don't see the trash on the streets.

Nothing is worth seeing trash/turds on streets. Nothing, when my own home is paradise and neat.

It's an emotional draught and a mental one. These are emotional illnesses that result, no fun.

A society who puts freedom first will end up with both: greater freedom and greater equality.

The bigotry they fight is the bigotry they promote. Duke Pesta

Instead of traveling spend your money on moving to a safe place or if you stay, on gates and fencing.

College was pure chaos and indecency and loud yelling and chicanery and I hated it believe me.

Haha: Even the soaps talk all about the glories of Paris, it's worth it to them to fool us on this.

Though they dominate everything, Trudeau says the problem is "white supremacy", oh come on.

China mocked the "little potato" Justin Trudeau but gave full honors to Trump, the highest to bestow.

Trudeau is an animal-hater and cruel. He okayed bestiality, unleashing hell and progressive fools.

Just when it seems impossible, the problems endless, God sends you a genius and instant success.

GLOBAL

"Worldly" they call themselves. Smug conceit, huffy arrogance: open the borders to all she says.

They're not our enemies but we have our own people to consider. Send them back/protect em there.

Obama and Trudeau: banal cliches to uncritical audiences.

Both Trudeau and Obama preferred foreign countries to their own.

You can no longer say that the west's values of biblical morality are superior, but they are.

Western demoralization brought loss of hope then low birth rate and then population replacement.

Mankind's asleep hypnotized by mantras of group beliefs but you've got God Almighty, how neat.

Their plan was to make us hopeless and they did a good job cuz we stopped replacing ourselves.

Should be concerned about Canada since it's the same continent/a northern border needed.

What you see as freedom we see as moral degradation.

It's not about utopia but stopping globalist's dystopia and moving forward for a great again America.

After Merkel Madness we wonder if female intelligence has regressed for they sure create messes.

Oprah's part of world government to curb world population so who do you think is behind this notion?

GLOBAL

Don't believe multiculturalism works--they are just kowtowing to minorities with whites shirked.

Oprah is the chosen black face of African sterilization and abortion while getting rid of men.

Women aren't nationalistic cuz it's male to wanna progress his thing, only through patriotism.

Women tend to suckup to government and react emotionally--thus the globalism abomination.

Yes, we do have a problem with Islamophobia--it's a made-up word by leftist crazies like you.

It's a Judeo-Christian country at it's core and they can't stand it/want it dead and gone forever.

Oprah is the Judas goat to lead Africa into sterilization and it's all part of the eugenics program.

This Oprah episode has brought eugenics globalism to light--she's just the head jerk of this blight.

Global.Islam is communistic: an elite group at the top then us poor devils. Want: capitalistic.

The Merkel Call led to a stampede.

I feel such sympathy for Germany. Imagine the terror as hordes plow through your property.

Males are nationalists to protect their interests but women are emotional, relating to concepts.

GLOBAL

Nothing but evil: Calling Austrians Nazis cuz they want to live in peace, harmony and security.

Merkel is the epitome of the dangers of feminism, letting one incompetent ruin a continent.

A man guards his own interests thru nationalism, not some unelected board unrelated to him.

Just America, not unelected boards (full immunity and tax exemption) with a globalist agenda.

Get out, why would we want all those people here? Liberals never think of that, just listen to peers.

They can't stand Trump cuz he's practical. They're used to pie in the sky utopian ideological.

"Austria's Nazi past raises it's head" while it shoulda read: "saved from Germany's blight" instead.

Look at core women ruining nations: Clinton, May, Merkel--solid proof of destructive feminism.

What a nightmare as conquered Germany is daily punished by the spiteful harridan at the helm.

Can you imagine frustration of Germans, but due to Hitler guilt feel they deserve comeuppance?

Never trust a woman who's not a nationalist because they tend to suckup to globalist governments.

People are rising up against this evil, rejecting leftist ideology and their backers the globalist elite.

GLOBAL

Happy Austrians: "We want to keep our values, culture and traditions intact"

In Germany, being called "Nazi" shuts you up quickly.

The whole bloody plan was to substitute Muslim populations for votes in tolerant liberal nations.

They knew we'd put up with this, all for their number one value: TOLERANCE.

Merkel's 15-second answer to civilian terror: "fear's not a good adviser".

ISIS said they'd sneak in with migrants, pres.

Feminists love the conquistadors who are cruel, horrible, debauched, inbred, dumbed, entitled.

Merkel says to deal with your fears, "go see a painting in a church" and that's the feminist leader.

All that matters is mass illegal immigration and no other issue takes precedence for this nation.

Another feminist fraud destroying her nation. Theresa May blames whites for multicultural problems.

You know multiculturalism has failed with Theresa May alters crime stats to make everyone equal.

White people are the sacrificial lambs so leaders can paint a picture of multicultural success.

An opportunity to see our way was right/superior but a threat to globalists putting us to the rear.

GLOBAL

Bash/debase the whites rather than tell the uncomfortable truth: invaders cruel and uncouth.

Dearly beloved, the leftists and Islamic aggression against Christianity and our nation is serious.

Blindly welcomed migrants to Europe and in turn brought violence and terror to the continent.

Flooded with strangers you will lose your identity, culture, traditions, values and sense of reality.

Imagine being flooded with strangers in your house. Make it personal, bring it down, it's a louse.

Like an abused dog we collapse in the corner, waiting to die as they know we will, without mourners.

Your devices of deception like Media, Hollywood, U.N., NASA and Planned Parenthood are exposed.

You're exposed, your Luciferian reign is over.

EU Order: Open your borders and surrender your cultures.

The migrant relocation scheme was forced thru the EU in 2015, though not one nation agreed.

Civics is the fix.

EU and Soros want to Muslimize Europe.

Any EU punishment is more desirable than letting these people in.

Mental disorders run rampant in the EU hierarchy.

GLOBAL

Trudeau and Macron are other pretty boys out to destroy.

Liberal artists pride themselves as "citizens of the world" but the highest is patriotism for your own.

We must become isolationist or we get too sick. It's a terrible shock and why should we? Resist.

It's normal to wanna be around people like you. Similitude! Multiculturalism isn't just about food.

The mere fact you can tolerate that crap means you're a loser and cuck.

We don't want em here: kill dogs throw gays off roofs stone women rape children, we hate their guts.

It's an evil, sick ideology.

Personal freedom vs. being thrown in with em! Like rats in a cage, the worst possible congerin'

Be an atheist just cuz you hate false religion? Question this.

Trudeau's hopes are to offset his tanking popularity with immense immigration increase.

Merkel hates Germany as Obama did America.

There are competent female leaders, rare nationalists. But generally it's politics vs. female intelligence.

We can't allow feminists to destroy the world which Merkel's trying to--naive or a witch's brew?

Kurz (closed-borders nationalist) won Austria over a feminist who woulda opened borders to all of ya.

GLOBAL

Poland wants it's own culture, traditions and identity--it takes spine to be free.

Whites are the only ethnicity not allowed pride: In terms of "diversity" this is the Great Lie.

It is massive incompetence allied with a sense of historical guilt and self-negation or dislike.

It's not "diversity" it's non-whites ganging up on whites.

The clear can't understand--like the wise--why liberal females love a medieval doctrine of women's rights.

Diversity + proximity = war.

The west has betrayed all the values that made it great and now we're allowing this mean fate.

West is massively importing low IQ populations.

Anytime you have a large group of unmarried men in society you have trouble, planned for Europe.

Women vote for larger government and open borders so when looking for a reason look at hers.

Women love welfare, open borders and the more immigrants the better.

The fact women want open borders means we never shoulda made em voters.

Liberals all for gay rights but then bring in people who hang em high.

Feminist miffed due to disrespect ends up marrying wifebeater--same contradiction as the border.

GLOBAL

Women are attacking white men, siding with enemies and inviting them in/no loyalty to husbands.

Women treat their men with contempt while worshipping the most sexist group possible: enigmatic.

What's this bull that immigration brings prosperity for all? Don't you know 90% are on the dole?

They don't come for values but the money values produced, then the giant welfare state ensues.

The values of the west were science, reason, values of free market and medicine, capitalism.

Just cuz something is legal doesn't make it right. Look at the crap Trudeau legalizes in middle of night.

It all seems self-evident to the shallow mind who can't think deeply. Communism never works, truly.

Globalists' endgame is no family/church so they have total control-- government worship by y'all.

They killed Levoy Finicum because he spoke for the ranchers and miners devastated where I live.

He loved freedom, his agency given by God.

They wanna take the land so they denounce family, creed, patriotism and the true woman or man.

Dumb love war/destruction, smart love refinement/devotion: the west's grossification was it's end.

GLOBAL

Can you imagine beautiful Europe flooded and destroyed by antiChristian vandals? It's happening now.

All of the historical treasures of Europe will be destroyed not just taken over, cuz they aren't Islam.

Won't stop at destroying church icons, it'll be old castles too cuz those are bad and must be gone.

Beautiful treasure of Europe, subsumed and totally unappreciated, destroyed without letup.

It's to restructure the fabric of society--social engineering--and there's nothing you can do about it.

Communism: cold-blooded plans without consideration for you and your clan and it's horrible, man.

There are no lone wolves, in the global Jihad there are only soldiers. Pamela Geller

Muslim gangs surround a woman and rape her until she's dead or disabled and feminists say all-ok.

If they're a hundred times more violent of course we're scared, avoid or walk the other way.

Sweden is the epitome of pathological altruism.

An introduction to communism and what it's all about: killing off those who don't fit/go along with it.

For people who don't know a darn thing communism is the in-thing.

Communism made simple: Ultimate harmony is only reached after certain groups of people are killed.

GLOBAL

They literally can't see--it's a mental illness. That's what Jesus meant about these blind guides.

Don't you want freedom to move about, do what you want? Communism is tyranny, a cage, a drought.

You going along with this, Che/Castro shirts, even Mao--now you've gone too far/we see who you are.

Sick freaks home from school trashing Trump and saying communism is cool. P.S. They're also cruel.

Tried to start race wars targeting white people. Brought the 3rd world in slyly to make it all equal.

Liberals are about sharing all you have--communism--and they'll invade you to get it, man.

Here you're paying all that tuition and they come home putting you down/spouting communism?

It's all a bloody idea, just like Islam has bloody borders. Make em conform or millions are goners.

Your krazy kollege kids are wearing Stalin or Che shirts and you're paying big bucks for a giant curse.

You're paying big bucks so they can destroy us saying open borders are best: wake up to these pests!

Top intellectuals, best workers and engineers: they will kill them all for society's total restructure.

To communists killing is essential.

GLOBAL

They sell multiculturalism through our senses: the pleasure of the eyes, ears, colors and tastiness.

Bright happy colors and promises of dictators and the communists--see that's how they get us.

Without a return to what made the west great, all of the capitals of western Europe will fall.

No, we ended slavery. No, it was the democrats who were slaveowners. No, crusades were defensive.

Yes they're nice but without Christian ethics always lotsa backstabbing, gossip and secret vice.

Social Marxism is touted as the default moral position so women chant on in empathy illness.

The insanity of denial in Sweden, the epitome of pathological altruism and it is white genocide ma'am.

Conflating Islam with race (brown skin) has immunized it from all criticism.

Whole world: left is crushing the right (family, town, religion, tradition) by this Trojan horse blight.

This bloody Islamic invasion (which means the death of millions) is so epic it's of historic proportions.

It's just human nature when politicians are bought/paid for and multiplied across world means it's over.

So you say all cultures are alike--you'll find out real fast how wrong you are thru the crime hike.

GLOBAL

 If you're fragile, don't travel. How people romanticize leaving comfy homes makes me marvel.

All we can do is comment as ship goes down. It's catastrophic but what can we do but frown?

The pope is a globalist traitor helping to destroy Europe thru mass immigration.

Thousands dead, hundreds killed per attack. And nowhere in the media does it say it's Islamic.

We can't get thru to leftists let alone a mob of em. Even terror attacks don't do it, they double down.

Mass immigration from third world nations equals white genocide and losing our life stations.

Paris Syndrome is culture shock, add London or California Syndrome and the moral is: stay home!

Paris Syndrome after-effects are very real--so utterly traumatized by the experience revealed.

Paris image: aesthetic haven, supermodels, tranquil beauty but the mean waiters shatter it instantly.

Racial realists are the real racists. We're not all the same, some are smart but many are asses.

Sweden is so sick they can't say "lord" or "He" for that would be deference to One higher than "we".

Racist, white nationalist, ethno-nationalist, identitarian, white advocate-- there's nothing wrong with it.

GLOBAL

This happened to make us proud of our whiteness. We were complacent, guilty, sinful, we lost it.

If we don't get group pride for whiteness we'll be slaughtered cuz that's what's on the burner.

We understand them but they do not and cannot understand us and that's why we gotta get up.

These people are not like you. You only hang with them cuz you're scared, lonely, hypnotized, blue.

There's a very wide gulf between us and them. It's all social engineering and a longterm plan.

All these invaders: I'm scared to death! I'd be a fool not to have fear from all I've watched and read.

Don't believe the guff we're all equal--that's a bunch of bull. Check things like IQ why don't you.

Stop accepting white-bashing cuz it's something you live up to/be proud of, we built civilization man.

They put us down for everything, they want everyone brown. We were the builders, we ran the farms.

We built Europe, Christians channeling God. But men are cuckholded and won't fight for it, how odd.

Slavery by whites was 100 years, slavery by black Muslims all thru history-- horrible acts by monsters.

Mausoleum of scum: Oprah the globalist tool-bag actually says she stands for victimized women.

GLOBAL

The biggest victims currently are white men. Having lost real male identity they just keep dwindlin'

Just look at the stuff the white man built, and now they're the most victimized by guilt?

Ploy: to take down the best to then even and divvy up the whole world by destroying the west.

Yes, there needs to be a resurgence of white nationalism, and it's life-saving pride, not racism.

True racism is wanting what is best for your own race and seeing the differences in all races.

Oprah: Create crisis, manage crisis.

Research Oprah's tax exemption, the UN and other things she's involved in then be chagrined.

Oprah is a beautiful woman (smart with spirit) but joined the wicked to control the people (fear it).

Stay strong as they'll be force feeding us Oprah, the face of black depopulation and abortion.

White men always ran militaries so is it karma this current degradation, from past wars? Perhaps

IQ is like height--despite some environmental factors they won't be taller than genetics allows.

The globalists want low cognitives who can't handle complexity cuz they won't question see.

GLOBAL

They see no differences between genders, ethnicities or races and it's painful as scientists.

My women's party went dead silent when I admired president elect and dispelled Oprah worship.

"Racism" used to explain everything (but it doesn't) vs. genetic differences, teachers or peasants.

Tearing ourselves up finding scapegoats for disparities when the facts speak for themselves, truly.

Most churches have been bought off and compromised. They're for sin, amnesty and Soro's lies.

Justin Trudeau, an actor and Soro's puppet, is destroying Canada and they can't do a thing about it.

Of course not all but most women are dumbed by social hypnotism, suckers for fake news/globalism.

Feminism: globalist scheme to wimp the men, not help women you fools! You're pawns, not cool.

When women break from the liberal hypnotic they become the smartest and most nationalistic.

Everyone gets something free if they vote for Oprah Winfrey.

Oprah is a billionaire who wants to shrink world pop--she's a member of the whole stinking club.

Why wouldn't you want to help your own countrymen not foreigners you've nothing in common with?

Feminists love those who push gays off buildings/are ok with stonings and they aren't phonies?

GLOBAL

You can't expect more from people than their gene codes allows.

To believe that you'd have to be low IQ so I'm through.

Globalists use Cloward-Piven strategy to make us all poor so they can dictate the terms of surrender.

Build that wall, deport them all. Build that wall, deport them *all!* Michael Savage

Sanctuary cities violate federal law. Trump: send in the troops, make em comply and do it now!

Where is your outrage, jerk? There is none unless useful to your liberal agenda ("they're here to work").

California controlled by front groups for the Mexican government, nothing we can to do about it.

Mexican bum kills young girl and there is no fine, no prison time. San Francisco: feces/crime.

Mexican bum kills young girl and he goes free: San Francisco home of crime and feces.

Human life has no value in the liberal world: Kill babies and when bums shoot ladies they go free.

Investigate his shyster lawyer for jury fixing, but the whole system is a Mexican/globalist conspiracy.

Liberal cities: corruption and feces.

Libs say illegals come here to work: they're better than us natives--more deserving of perks.

The most important thing is to feel virtuous so they spout nonsense despite the dangerous.

Sweden is an "humanitarian superpower" so now she's flooded with migrants and it's like a sewer.

Despite mass rapes the majority in Sweden still want an open door policy, thus this current tragedy.

The masochism of the west knows no bounds at all. Tucker Carlson

If a Swedish rape victim speaks out the feminists will hunt her down--more on the insanity of liberalism.

To the Swedish feminists the migrants can do no wrong even gang rapists.

Swedish feminists applauding gang rapists are the biggest example/proof liberalism is a mental illness.

World War Two, Nazi guilt swept Europe, susceptible to liberal garbage and now swallowed up.

Globalists know about Nazi guilt--they created it--so they know such insults work/we can see it.

There's an absolute belief Sweden's a multicultural utopia and they're stuck in this tragic myopia.

Sweden would rather destroy their own country than be called racist.

Theresa Mae said "London Muslims don't do terrorism, right-wingers do" so she's letting it go, soon.

Sweden is also known as the "feminist capital of the world"--how ironic as mass gang rapes unfurl.

GLOBAL

We don't have a right to big house/land, gotta bring people in: that's the communist spirit man.

You don't have that right to enjoy your land and big house. You gotta bring em all in you louse.

Paris Syndrome: Travelers' extreme shock at realizing Paris was nothing what they thought.

Just like Merkel she wants to help people and doesn't care who gets hurt in the process: liberals!

She has a communist spirit: she doesn't want you to enjoy all that privacy and room, she'll bring em in.

Once the dominoes start to fall there's no stopping them. It can work either way but we want freedom.

Islam killed 100 million Hindus, no wonder Indians love Trump.

What, men will stand by and watch girls raped rather than be called "racist"? I can't believe this.

Church is a huge part of the New World Order. It's incredible since the bible lays it out as the warner.

The churches are supposed to pastor us Americans. But instead for money they flood us with aliens.

The progressives are just overreaching environmental activists pushing their own narratives.

Globalists want to sabotage the west so they bring in armies of it's enemies who think tyranny is best.

GLOBAL

 Very clever bringing in armies of young men to kill the west but we're all effected in this game of chess.

Chain migration is how the democrats increase new votes exponentially and even geometrically.

Crap hole defined: Third world place without plumbing. Haiti.

Any place democrats rule are hellholes and crapholes.

The parasitic creatures are all mad their scams are falling down and thus they all hate Trump.

Even as he crushed ISIS and exploded our economy in this crisis the silly liberals still hate his guts.

The forces of atheistic godless globalism are in retreat.

Stop remorse and start thinking about what you can do for society. End maudlin self-reproach, truly.

How bizarre the merging of the far left idiotics with Islamic modesty culture in sexualizing kids.

If Trump commits amnesty treachery we will never forgive him and will hate his guts while losing freedoms.

DACA is the dividing line with this president. If he betrays his base then watch out, we'll be bent.

If Trump exchanges amnesty for the wall then they have the votes to make it ineffective, that's all.

We got you in to get all these people out, Trump!

The two biggest troublemakers are the churches and women who say "open borders, let em all in".

GLOBAL

Globalism seems an intuitive thing. It's like a tautology, appearing logical with a self-evident ring.

I was wrong about global warming. Al Gore

Dogs are being slaughtered by the millions to adapt to (not offend) the Muslims so speak out man.

There is a subtle awakening among all white people--decent Christians are scorned as evil.

These people don't live like we do. They believe totally differently and most hate dogs too.

Nothing wrong with loving your own, wanting to be around just them, so ignore liberals--they're done.

You wanna let other cultures in here to ruin everything we've created from Christian capitalism sir.

A measure of a humane culture is how they treat dogs so that leaves out Islam, please help us God!

Due to Christian restraint we take a lot of sh*t until that moment comes when you've had it.

Liberal culture is always the same litany of persecution, oppression and chip on the shoulder.

Realize: Everything Oprah does is to get women to sign on to the UN to be disempowered and sterilized.

Oprah has a world church to brainwash children and it's called the "good club" cuz it's evil sin.

Oprah is an absolute anti-human Nazi troll.

GLOBAL

Listen to a racial realist to get escape from the mind-numbing prevailing orthodoxy of diversity.

We never said we were superior, just different.

Europe: Kindness to strangers is cruelty to their own children but so far they haven't learned.

The "white privilege" button is just greed and exploitation of us: morally sensitive groups.

Transfer our funds to minorities is all about feeling good, relieving guilt and getting voters.

Colleges: if you want real diversity hire a race realist or how about just an ordinary conservative?

Humans are tribal with a natural preference for people like themselves. Why force diversity hell?

They took over our country and now we're a despised minority?

Instead of recognizing the present catastrophe we've turned it around to "diversity is strength" baloney.

Diversity is a source of three things: conflict, tension and hostility.

Diversity kills trust. Wars result from diverse people living in the same territory, there's always a fuss.

"Diversity is our strength" is just a slogan which can't rewrite the laws of nature/inevitable bickering.

Whites applauding diversity are committing suicide cuz it means replacing Europeans with non.

GLOBAL

Merkel with her unmitigated gall says measures to stop these killings "defy our European values".

Luxembourg motto: "We want to remain what we are"--what a quaint idea to love your own forever.

Whites are waking up everyday to this ghastly anti-white nightmare and the terrible price we pay.

The white's unwillingness to have children is the direct result of the anti-white ambience all around.

We don't have to deport--just pull the plug and they'll all just leave, but we don't do this of course.

Speak out now so future generations won't think we were all cowards and fools. Guillaume Faye

Thanks to those like Jarad Taylor there's been an explosion of white racial consciousness/determinism.

What's it gonna take for whites to defend their own interests? Have we been so neutered, masochists?

Egalitarian orthodoxy is dying but like all wounded animals is putting up a tremendous fighting.

We are supposed to be bowing our heads to non-whites rather than to God. Jarad Taylor

More Muslims, more killings, and France and Germany is stuffed with em as bodies keep piling.

Pull the plug/cut benefits and they'll all stay home and less will die on the routes/in the boats.

GLOBAL

Isn't it funny how peaceful leftists turn to violence reacting to an obvious question or hard facts?

The biggest issue is immigration and that's what wins elections so the dems wanna bring em in.

If a politician is open to it of course foreign governments will come in and buy off national resources.

Western values are universal values, adopted here but not there. They are superior.

If whites valued European heritage they'd have many more children but that's not the case.

Lincoln fought to free blacks but afterwards wanted them deported—an undisputed historical fact.

Coyotes: ten grand a head to smuggle em in.

Trump wants to be "flexible" while waiting for an "agreement" but doesn't that mean letting em all in?

We elected you to stop flow of illegals into country, Trump. If you vote for DACA we'll throw you out.

Fake to the left?

The real "dreamers" are the Americans who voted for Donald Trump with a vision of a renewed nation.

Socially engineered media narratives (cut and dry, carefully designed) for 5-second attention spans.

A technocratic mono-state: same ideology with updated technology.

Theresa Mae appeasin' the fray

GLOBAL

Don't get too sure of yourself cuz trouble may come. There are always humblers, stay sweet son.

World War III is immigration, immigration, immigration.

Define projection: Though they did nothing we still feel tortured by them. But it's reality friends.

Immigration is the litmus test for politicians, separating mice from men.

Do not buy a robot dog for it can be hacked and programmed to kill you/can't be stopped.

All our lives, mesmerized by the most beautiful city in the world and here it's a mean trash bin too.

We feel tortured by em tho' they did nothing but it's still a feeling so I'd reject and get moving.

Any society that puts equality ahead of freedom will end up with neither. Dr. Milton Friedman

Though prime minister of Canada smokes pot, never heard of it making you that crazy, rot!

Why do elites gravitate to dictators? The Trudeaus just loved em--like Castro of the biggest killers.

Soros seeks to destroy us so why are we putting up with this?

Trudeau Sr.: hippie using the power of government to expand so-called civil rights for citizens.

Trudeau had youth, popular rhetoric, Trudeaumania from dad, hated conservative opposition.

GLOBAL

Trudeau admired/visited Castro as a kid. Hearing all about rights of all citizens (Islamo/communism).

Trudeau tends to give lavish gifts, trips and tax breaks to his friends.

Pizza Hut, Kentucky Fried and Taco Bell owned by Chinese so they endorse anthem protests.

Never see em again, they mean nothing, consigned to hell.

EU coup: Poland/Hungary new Eastern block.

50% Moroccan youths are arrested for crimes.

Despite the blatant contradiction of feminism/gays vs. Islam, their link of hating America is higher ma'am.

If they stand for women's rights it's Islamophobic. So leave feminism and for Islam applaud quick.

Five white people (old) are killed each week from black knockout games--they deserve it they say.

How wonderful: Coastal liberals putting up with homelessness, feces everywhere, illegals.

Human flow into Europe of biblical proportions.

The human flow is composed of economic migrants, refugees and foreign fighters.

The elites like Trudeau have more in common with authoritarian tyrants than the Canadians.

My most admired nation is China, for their dictatorship--making decisions on the spot. Justin Trudeau

GLOBAL

It's population replacement, liberal voter recruitment, massive virtue signaling, Soros destabilization.

Multiculturalism goes hand in hand with victim culture.

England is the most tolerant of Islam and the most hated by them.

The values of the majority are illegitimate cuz they exclude minorities: dangerous idea indeed.

Soros has lost many nations so has taken Trudeau under his wing and that means payin him.

New wave of protests Europe/UK may signal a reversal of the inevitability of populations replaced.

Islamophobic laws in Canada casts an incredibly wide and undefined net, as bad as it gets.

Liberalism: Third world can do no wrong and is the victim of the First which deserves whatever happens.

Many millions want in so once they reach a certain number they won't be able to resist the rest.

Paris: city of love is burned to the ground and filled with scum.

Just cuz I love middle eastern sounds doesn't mean I want mass illegal immigration of Muslims.

Middle Eastern Chill you'd call it, it's got that beat--but not to lose my culture, security and safety.

And just cuz I love salsa/latin sounds doesn't mean I want em from the south if they don't love dogs.

GLOBAL

You can have globalism so long as it's bottom-up not top-down.

It's sickening when Christians slide in with the majority view and our culture continues to dilute.

If fact I wish you'd all get out cuz we're the best/that's why you're here so be nice to dogs, please.

It's how they treat dogs--the least of us--that is a barometer of a culture so now go and figure.

Paris scum: Jihadis, military age men wanting to kill us, dumbed and Sharia is what they want.

To Hollywood scum, Trump restores economy = BAD. Oprah and Meryl defends sodomy = GOOD.

Oprah is the only black person in the original eugenics group funding Hitler and #1 enemy of blacks, sir.

Oprah is the "uniter" as she chirps men are horrible, Trump is evil, the media is wonderful.

Christmas ads include Muslims when they don't even celebrate it. Things are diluting, believe it.

Mohammed said women were "evil, stupid, unsuccessful, dirty, inferior and can be beaten."

They come for the money not the values that created the money.

They always pick on the least dangerous to bribe the strongest/most dangerous, think of that.

Wise rulers of the past finally said "kill em, kill em all" and God sometimes said that too you know.

GLOBAL

The whole world should recognize Merkel for the mass murderer she is but ignorance is bliss.

It is so horrible, these people are animals! They are lower, even animals don't act like this.

Tragic genetic differences between groups but it's no one's fault.

Justin Trudeau loves Castro who killed the same proportion of Cubans as Stalin did of Russians.

The migrant invasion is the European left as American democrats plot to import third world crap.

They want the votes and to crush the right for good and it's all about maintaining power/affluence.

Merkel is like someone opening your door and letting a big gang in for whatever they want you for.

Merkel apparently can't see how she's murdering her own people, more virtue signaling/Nazi guilt.

Globalism is heartless capitalism while masses are poverty-stricken.

Hard to see the monstrosity you're capable of (can do damage to the soul) but it's necessary to know.

It's not so much you but weakness reflecting the collective unconscious and lower archetypes.

I can't believe you'd actually choose that over us--are you nuts?

It's a 100 year plan to bring us down thru demoralization then invasion by antithetical cultures.

GLOBAL

Only 8% of Canadians want this immigration yet that's his main thing, entirely non-legit.

Trudeau is the biggest globalist stooge today as he brings em all in and demoralizes his country.

Kurz banned Soros from Austria, Trudeau takes his orders from this traitor to Europe/Canada/America.

Trudeau's mentor is the richest traitor in the world--that accounts for his haughty self-satisfied smirk.

31 year old Kurz booted Soros out and won't let one in, in the middle of a surrounding EU trash bin.

The youngest leader in the world Kurz won't let one in cuz he's saving his culture, family and friends.

Trump has done way more than save America--he's a beacon to many others following in step.

Everyone wants to know Daddy believe me, he's the king as the leftists are perverted, crazy, shady.

The youngest leader knows what's going on but most others are stodgy, bought, low IQ ideologues.

The fact Canadians voted in an actor with no experience shows liberalism is a mental illness.

He looks good, talks in happy platitudes and that is all it takes for the dense and lazy multitudes.

Big daddy Soros behind him so he feels bloated with self-satisfaction but don't worry God'll get him.

GLOBAL

Kurz is better looking than Trudeau, a mishap--take that you lame ass piece of crap. Katie Hopkins

Trudeau is fascinating/hilarious were it not so tragic what he's is doing to a land so history-rich.

They said we couldn't discipline our kids now they say no fences or gates preparing for our slaughter.

The feds have the power to retry this case and Trump's government will confront this disgrace.

Disgraceful verdict for Kate Steinle! No wonder Americans are so angry with Illegal Immigration. Trump

Greedy and corrupt California has melted down under Jerry Brown, it's like Venezuela or a mafia town.

The illegal bum who killed Kate Steinle is now a folk hero to the hard left. Can you imagine that?

Evil fairytale: Kill a white woman and you're free, kill a sea lion and it's 100 grand/a year in jail, see?

Trump can send in the troops and if the locals don't comply throw em in jail. Otherwise, evil prevails.

Kate's murder ignored/acquitted: family grief. When used as a "political football": liberals' great relief.

California (in fact, both coasts) stink. Get out while you still can, we're marching towards the brink.

London is California, Clinton and De Blasio's New York. The rest of UK is good, decent, hard at work.

They sacrifice everything to multiculturalism and remain deep in delusion during our destruction.

CHRISTIAN IS A HUMBLE BUILDING

They're not interested in a humble little building like the Baptist church, they want extravagance.

No Christian fashion shows just restraint and modesty, that's all--not making it hip/trendy for y'all.

The more lowminded the more impressed with Satan's tactics of splendor and empty promises.

They think operatic extravagance equals God, but Jesus was a humble man not a pharisaic slob.

People are so shallow/unspiritual, attracted by the fantastic mosques and cathedrals, ya know.

They gotta see it to believe it--flashy mosque or cathedral makes it legit to the spiritually unfit.

Jesus is believing the the unseen--but we know Him, the tomb is empty and He's our only Reality.

They pray to nobody, he doesn't exist but billions are controlled somehow in this Satanic twist.

America took pride in decency cuz we started as Puritans. We had lines, respect, sense, manners.

Our founders warned: these freedom principals won't work unless you maintain morality not shirk it.

I wore ethnic clothes and enjoyed world music but now want American and avoid the tragic.

GLOBAL

There's nothing more evil than globalism cuz it's just numbers to them: plots and takeover plans.

Oprah's show was to target American whites with mind control and women ate it up (lost their soul).

The safest place for women and children to be is in a marriage which Oprah type feminists only disparage.

Good riddance cuz I'm sick of your false religious proclamations and self-serving rantings.

Twisted souls seeking to make greater men or women their slaves.

The liberal losers are out of their league with this queen, definitely. She's as smart as Trump, truly.

When attacked, Brits are to "run, hide and tell"--how unrecognizable and wimpish to real men of WWII.

After terror the media machine goes into action, terrifying to observe as they've lost all nerve.

60,000 white farmers cleansed by blacks in Africa--happening everywhere not just America.

Lower IQ, communication skills, semantical lexicon and dialect (vocabulary). Isolated, no talk.

The acculturation process is such that people are totally unique in different eras, places, cultures.

If you're fascinated with human differences, go into cultural anthropology or psychology and see it.

GLOBAL

 Mass migration masquerading as humanitarian cause but it's true nature is occupation of territory.

Migrants change the character of our country and we don't want our country's character changed.

Whether they sterilize us or kill us thru chemtrails it's all the same bunch of fellas so get hep, get real.

Our survival depends on changing people's minds to think like us and when enough do, success.

What makes this so tragic is the people engineering our displacement is our own flesh and blood.

We live in two different worlds psychologically and that makes it impossible to share a world physically.

If white people are "hopeless" ok fine let us build our own hopeless societies free of interruption.

Fascinating. To African friends: is it true the African language cannot include vows, promises, future, past?

The most impacted/crowded states from illegals is Ca, Tex, Fl, NY, NJ and Illinois and it's terrible guys.

Looking at the comments, increasingly more whites are seeing it for the embarrassing insanity it is.

Globalists want totally poor people living in coffin apartments so of course they hate Trump the best.

Even Haitians hate Haiti--do you think Trump is right maybe?

If Obama won't take holiday in Haiti he's a racist.

GLOBAL

White parents withdrawing kids from colleges cuz they hate spineless groveling cowards running em.

The more they take over our country the more terrified you are to say what you think, so you drink.

Speak! Because the more you speak the less cowards are cowardly cuz they sense others agree.

It's the censorship that gives us total skepticism about anything coming down from above.

When you are all by yourself it's lonely but if four or five of you it's a movement, so get going.

CNN got off on saying "shit hole" 1200 X in a week.

Studies show those who live in diverse neighborhoods don't trust neighbors and are not involved.

All studies show Muslim immigrants get more radicalized not more integrated as time goes on.

White men supplanted and then forced to remain invisible in their own country until they die.

When you have power give it to me cuz it's your principal. When I have it, I'll take yours cuz it's mine.

You must not massacre us cuz it's not your custom. But we will massacre you cuz it's ours, and fun.

Any news on TV is globalist, save a few. I'd give it all up and select what you study, good for you.

GLOBAL

Higher IQ means refinement, restraint, mildness, gentleness but don't get us mad you finks.

They don't wanna go home cuz they want to live in white societies where things are nice.

Biggest liberal myth in all history: all races are alike, it's just illusory.

Show me a multi-racial society and I'll show you conflict. Jarad Taylor

So let me see: You and your liberal cronies want to become a hated minority in your own country?

West was built by Faustian individualism but when surrounded by groupies it becomes a problem.

Non-whites have group solidarity and we do not--must change this now or be cast out as rot.

When they start that s**t say "so you want us to be a hated minority in our own country, is that it?

So you want us to be welcoming to y'all while for us pieces of the pie are cut more small?

So to get money outa me you exploit my good graces/white guilt making me feel bad and shady?

It's OK to love your own people and superior European traditions and history and to hate evil!

It's OK to want to stop this mess for the sake of your own family and it's extension, our country.

Go to hell you liberal white cuckholds gladly giving away what my ancestors built for us, we, me!

GLOBAL

What we're pist off about is the wall and deportations aren't happening fast enough as promised.

What we're pist off about is they're flooding in at Obama levels when we don't even want anymore *legals!*

Did you know how many blacks are glad, relieved and happy to hear about race IQ differentials?

You see, they came here cuz they like white society so much better than the hell holes, a fetter.

Who wants to live in a trash-filled shit hole defined as a third world country without plumbing?

Whites need pride in shared traditions, heritage, family, history, victories and achievements.

No other country lets foreigners in to put their snouts in the troughs. Jarad Taylor

That's what gave it charm--the unique differences, now crushed and overrun by inferior: facts.

Why are they the inferior? Because they're coming here (on the dole) and we ain't going there.

We're not taking in their best who could do us some good. It's they're lazy usually, dead wood.

Dysgenic birth rate: Low IQ *many*, high IQ *few*.

If "race doesn't exist" how come racism is everywhere? Jarad Taylor

If you don't have high boundaries it's something you're gonna have to learn the hard way, truly

FASTER

For a fertile mind stop eating.

For me, one meal means one *exposure* a day. Two meals means acid and hell to pay.

Greatest weight loss tool ever: Eat a huge breakfast every day and be satisfied and happy forever.

Eat all you want for breakfast (be a hedonist) but then not one morsel (be a soldier and dead earnest).

Eat all you want then not one morsel! Now we go into assimilation and elimination/it all goes thru.

Three systems: digestion, assimilation, elimination. It's one or the other, so don't eat again brother.

Eat one morsel after breakfast and we go back into digestion and it all blocks up into constipation.

Forget dressing for dinner, skip it to be a winner. Just eat a big breakfast then fast to be thinner.

The mean globalists (trying to kill us) said "no butter" in the seventies and we all got fat and slovenly.

Give up the rabbit food and just eat pizza then be satisfied all day with strength for the arena.

The saddest thing was when naive ladies substituted margarine for butter--they died of cancer.

FASTER

We love cows and goats because we need them for our sustenance so don't listen to vegan nuts.

The merry love dairy cuz without it they're always hungry.

Breakfast-only plan for the saints or it's choking/acid at night, no gains.

The dogs and I have one feeding session in the morning. We fuel the tank then get to working.

We Americans are into butter, cream, cheese, raw milk, yogurt and that's it--we stay cute and fit.

The point is: we gotta eat. So what should it be? Lettuce, cauliflower, apples or things with substance?

Western breakfast: Starch, butter, eggs, maple syrup--they were hardiest so enjoy your French toast.

When I do eat (every 24-36 hours) it's most calorically dense--watery rabbit food makes no sense.

So you had bread and jam. Take joy for weight gain cuz now you've gotta fast three days, ma'am.

We change every decade and illness brings it on but is also an opportunity to turn it around.

Whenever you hit a glitch, switch--fast to overcome the witch.

Fasting breaks blocks in your environment or virtually. Across the world, wherever really.

Fasting to overcome is your trump card. Pull it for victory, do it now.

Prostate cancer is common then radiation and beach ball bellies so disabling. RX: Lactofrutarian then fasting.

FASTER

If your Total Load is down you can handle what comes around.

Cashmere. Makes me sick or it's suddenly ok because total load has changed.

Total Load: Food, environment, drugs, chemicals, emotional, stress--a constantly sliding variable, yes?

If your Total Load is up you're sick all the time as stimuli generalized.

First sign in me: bubbles and then acid. Get away, instant relief (reason for biggest industry, ant-acids).

It's just not worth it even to eat. Fill the tank in the morning then work, fly, enjoy cuz you're free.

It's ok but not every day: sensitives must rotate meals to be trim and stay that way, it's about allergy.

With allergy (not rotating your meals) you start to retain water and build a false body of blubber.

After detox you're more sick than ever unless stay in your bubble to endure chemicals or whatever.

It's not about any one diet but rotating meals to constantly bring balance and avoid allergy pitfalls.

Week: alternate cereal 2 days, pizza/tacos 2 days, rice noodles/ramen 2 days milk/ lactufruitarian, fast all day.

Rice noodles with veggies/salsa, tacos/cheese refreshes ya, raisin bran just cuz we love ya.

Just fuel the tank and don't get into it after that.

FASTER

The bad effects of types of foods is negated with reversal dieting. Just once is ok, it's fleeting.

The only answer is to get away from the stimulus. It's duration, intensity, proximity with us.

Don't listen to them—there is nothing wrong with cheese. Just go ahead and enjoy it, please.

Cheese is how they always stored milk for the winter. It and butter makes everything taste better.

Homemaking lesson of the 50's: Slim women making good use of delicious raw dairy for their families.

Delicious butter, raw milk, cream, cheese: The skinny ladies made good use of them it seems.

Isn't it funny that in this day we're supposed to avoid dairy and we're fatter than ever and lazy?

Skinny pretty Masai mostly live on dairy, no lie.

Cheese on crackers made of seeds please.

Life begins when dieting stops. Eat what you need, what you want. Carbs/fats together, looking gaunt.

What freedom not to restrict foods: no more diet dogma or bookish constraints of fools.

The more I relax/fast during the day the easier my work the next morning.

Whatever made me think God was wrong for food He made for man. Dieting/restricting is a demon.

FASTER

Is your carpet making you bilious? Just get away from the stimulus not call a doctor that's ridiculous.

DIP: duration, intensity, proximity. Reaction is a sliding variable not etched in stone you fool.

They think I lied because I could take it last night when other times I was sick: it's a variable that slides.

Immunity is based on one principal: total load. Bad diet makes it go up then I'm in reaction mode.

MCS is a fine science cuz they're flooding us with toxic chemicals then our reactions get worse.

Once you cross that line it feels like a gas chamber--gotta escape while before you were fine.

Beans are best with cheese, salsa, lettuce, tortilla and onion--that's us daily taco heads in the west.

We Americans love our big breakfasts after which we work all day long and become rich and famous.

It's a *humane* dairy, baby. These are our pets, they all have names and they are very happy.

Don't call it breakfast it's a fueling session.

Why do we put butter on top of vegetables? So we'll eat our veggies though we may not want to.

Diets will always bring you down because you're not *free* to eat what you please/what you need.

Eat everything in sight then skip lunch and dinner, increase your might.

FASTER

Why is everyone is so bloated? It's from the food and even if organic still the chemtrails getcha.

Hospitalized for an incident from hell God stripped him of fat, cancer, addiction to sleeping pills.

Aging is just latent disease--obstruction. Fast it out and you de-age through toxin-elimination.

Particulate dispersion remains in the air. These are chemtrails making us sick/bloated and it's not fair.

Being drunk is no excuse but it happens to be the truth as anosignasia sets in then we're through.

Beans and spuds, butter and cheese--what else is there? Raw milk and fruit smoothie please.

Pizza is just so much easier, then don't have to eat for 24 hours.

Pizza makes life so much easier, forget the greenhouse just store in freezer.

When you eat it's the most calorically dense cuz when will you ever eat again or have the chance?

If you eat again the cultural crap will make you ugly and fat but if it's just one meal a day, non-effect.

Liberal tyranny extended also to putting down our national foods: breakfast oats is not for fools.

Older women have saddlebags--and if thin they're very sexy: shows they've loved and lived/not hags.

Lack of walls was the basis for every problem I ever had.

FASTER

They want us dead, ugly, fat, aged, diseased, boring, noncreative, poor and hopefully suicided.

What to Mexican dogs eat? Tacos, tamales, etc. What do Asian dogs eat? Rice or noodles I'll betcha.

Butter: The more you eat the better. You'll have no appetite all day and the skin tone just glimmers.

The produce is great (essential) for delicious salsas/sauces but if it's just that there's no advances.

We put salsas/sauces on it so we'll eat it. We gotta eat so this makes it pleasing (strength not effete).

My breakfast as a 95 pound teen: Dozen eggs, pound bacon, 8 donuts smothered in butter, lotsa cheese.

Anorexia is an emotional illness to fill the unfillable. It occurs in dry mental droughts and fables.

The disease is not genetically determined except as a reaction to stress--an unexplained mess.

Grapecure: a few raisins when hungry.

Milk and raisins: raisin bran without the bran.

If you're weak or sheltered first then travel may evoke the worst--don't chance it, keep your purse.

He can't eat, but he can eat a few raisins which can be his permanent diet: Grapecure for Cancer.

Ray's on raisins. That's all I'll eat to reduce acid when famishin'.

FASTER

Optional: Fruit or tacos, noodles or potatoes. Now fast. Unless you're keto—have at it.

Daily Fasting suggested (Old Lady Diet): Huge smoothie in morning with raw milk and fruit.

You see em everywhere--radiation treatments create "beach ball bellies"--they're trying to kill us.

Raisin bran, raw milk and raisins all certified organic with sliced banana now daily fast: fantastic.

Best breakfast ever: big bowl raisin bran with raw milk/extra raisins/sliced banana now fast after.

If hungry, piece cheese (sharp cheddar is me) or crackers of seeds.

Add a chocolate bar to your healthy repertoire.

If eating once a day, raisin bran/extra raisins and maple syrup with raw milk won't cause weight gain!

My cats seem to be drug addicts the way they cry for catnip and panic when they don't have it.

Raisin bran with raw milk, banana and extra raisins on top. Eat once a day then universe opens up.

Get organic bran flakes and your own raisins cuz they cover those in canola oil for some reason.

Beans and rice--what else do you need? It keeps old people alive, it's best with salsa and spice.

Beans and rice with salsa on it, there you have it/or cheese with it.

FASTER

The aneurism made him weak so he got into pornography for a week.

Flu shots double chances of catching the flu.

Pollution wipes out benefits of exercise.

So-called health nuts say skip breakfast to extend the fast but I say to that: good luck while I have a blast.

Studies show 40% of "certified organic" is actually filled with most pesticides-- can you believe it?

After buttered toast with maple syrup, fast 48 hours no sweat.

Do you think that just cuz those papers and ink are in a box in the closet it doesn't make you sick?

Two pieces pizza, fast 20 hours.

Noodles even with cheese then fast to tomorrow--see?

Many get skinny with age as body naturally jettisons additional burdens, to soar in the time remainin'.

Add butter, go 36 hours. Eating again is being pulled down, powerless.

Extreme chemtrailing after Davos cuz that's how they get back you know.

Diet: Pizza or ice cream with best ingredients.

Keep your rabbit food I'm sticking to the most calorically dense then fast for the mood, that groove.

Keep your dietary restraint deleting whole categories, I'm gonna eat what I want then fast for glory.

FASTER

"Lunch with little, sup with less—better yet, go to bed supperless". Ben Franklin

Breakfast is the the most calorically dense cuz I never know when I'm gonna eat again.

The only time I don't feel twelve is in a gathering where they remind me how far my life has evolved.

Daily Joy Fast: Not one nut, chip or bite or acid's shot back into the gullet and I've had it.

2 brownies and a muffin I ate in the aft set me back as they stuck but I'll fast to get back on track.

If you must eat again let it be a raisin, grape or olive to bind acid--all fruit goes alkaline kid.

ice cream: Blend 10 bananas, bag frozen fruit, dates or coconut butter with raw milk, freeze in cups.

Ray lost 45 pounds eating my lactofruitarian ice cream, the only way I could get him to eat fruit.

Now we're eating like a Chinaman: mandarin oranges or ramen.

For safety: Preserve your wealth in safe investments (metal), go to a safe place and get healthy.

Fruit or Vegetables
As your body cleans out you may crave only fruit.
Go for it, fruitarians are ageless, alert, energetic,
cute—impervious to chemicals too.

EPILOGUE

How do you have a first world country with a third world population?

Most of the world is pretty darn mean. We were refined due to heritage and everyone wants that scene.

Social justice is orthodox, authoritarian and boring. The right is the new counterculture, soaring.

Nothing is less attractive than aging progressives still pretending they're hip, edgy or sexy.

Just wait, you progressives! There'll be a Tsunami of backlash against you for the mess we're in.

How is it rebellious to hate Trump, mimicking their corporate billionaire masters and their guff?

The liberal race-denying open-borders advocates have control of all systems: must accept it.

Race Denialism rules liberalism as it's part of oneism: "we are all one" from a silly sixties song.

Racial realism is the only ideology giving answers to the confused white youth in our nation.

It's the only ideology our ancestors would see as rational—not twisted, insane and laughable.

Our thinking even science has been twisted and tortured to be compatible with cultural Marxism.

EPILOGUE

So much evil been done by the leftwing baby boomer elites of Western Europe/we're so far gone.

Europe's police forces at the moment have been turned into social justice-dominant experiments.

Marxian global utopianism will go the way of all such experiments in history, yet a tragedy.

As it all falls down a power vacuum will emerge. Resist--why not want the best for your own, sir?

Whites as a group face existential threats completely unmatched in our history. Julian Langness

Globalist's goal: To eradicate all sense of shared identity or purpose.

Will Europe's proud heritage and culture slip away, replaced by Islamization, enslavement, death?

It's the most rational choice as ancestors/angels rejoice: to defend one's own people and race.

Suffering can either ignoble or cripple a people so now shun evil and stand high as a steeple.

Liberal twilight zone: Investigating crimes of illegals is now genocide--where has reason gone?

Whatever you have, better be ready to fight for it or someone will take it either for greed or survival.

The point is not race but being displaced.

Bible says not to mark up bodies like the heathen do with tattoos. Be happy with what God gave you.

EPILOGUE

What are you doing about white racism and becoming a hated minority in your own country?

It's not Christian to care more about foreigners than your own people--in fact, it's just plain evil.

Racial differences are a scientific fact but race denialism has taken over since humans can't face it.

White welfare states destabilize the basis of their own high civilization by reversing it's effects.

You planted the seed now just wait as God said He would prosper and meet your need.

When I'm off at noon it's gotta be music, can't track a movie or anything else like that: right brain only.

Start watching movie then I gotta stop it ten times to go outdoors and think for a couple hours.

Men are nationalists because it serves their own interests--this is obvious, the more local it is.

What idiot would want communism? Only the most shallow thinkers, the mentally ill or women.

To the liberal youth: When you're fifty or sixty you'll be a hated minority in your own country.

Higher education is no solution to current wage stagnation it's all about mass immigration.

We are deconstructing the enlightenment period, on the brink of a new dark era. Helmuth Nyborg

The effects of IQ can be subdued by political systems.

EPILOGUE

Don't betray yourselves and ancestors by the suicidal fundamentalism of the left, a curse.

Left is stuck in the futile conformity of social justice while we are bursting with energy and creativity.

It's not about racists--how ridiculous.

Left was raised in nothingness--no loyalty to family, nation, God--and apathy/shame to ancestors.

Millinnials don't care about nothing--anti-conviction. Boldly meet em with something--create friction.

Globalists have preyed upon the weakness and gullibility of youth to consolidate their power.

Leftist revolutionary identity of 50 years is now stale, boring, conformist, uncool as you can get.

The utopian vision of crazy hippies is now the dominant governing orthodoxy of the west.

The system opposing us masquerades as a humanitarian concern for human rights and stuff.

White guilt creates dark thoughts crippled by the lies we bought.

But that self-loathing, self-doubting mechanism of white guilt has made us deep and interesting.

Demographic change (immigration) always hurts the weak and vulnerable first, it's like a curse.

Some people wanna set you free and others wanna give you free stuff and it's opposite, all bluff.

EPILOGUE

 Democrats can't give you a good argument so they're just gonna import people who will go for it.

It's a transforming thing to behold white youth explode triumphant after so much cowering.

Only someone from an overpriced college could live in the theoretical/be so divorced from reality.

Groomed dictators are always smiling, in fact it's a sure sign. And you loved him, swine!

May think we're nice till we're not then watch out

Races are just local varieties--that's all they are--so how could a race denialist deny this?

For the first time in history the unfit are having more children than the fit.

It's an interplay as to how IQ is expressed through that political system or mental illness.

70% of divorces the females start, so now we see grandmothers slaving at Walmart.

We need separate homelands and with time--very soon--you'll find that out man.

With upsurge of decency/respectability think of the 74,000 White Africans killed quite recently.

For Jarad Taylor the price of dealing with constant attacks as a race realist was undeserved obscurity.

There's a high rate of sociopathy in public office cuz they know how to conceal themselves.

EPILOGUE

 **My race is my nation. Important maxim.**

There is no escape from our tribal nature: There will always be us and there will always be them.

For anyone born after 1980 the dominant orthodoxy was white guilt and thus created a tragedy.

Raised on hipster cynicism and degeneracy we chose instead traditionalism, honor, decency.

My, the insanity of late stage liberalism.

There is a tide in the affairs of men which taken at the flood leads to fortune. Shakespeare

Ours is the God of separation & order and that speaks of boundaries & borders.

Demography is destiny. Auguste Comte

Groups in stress become stronger/bonded in self-protection but their progeny loses this direction.

Groups get strong/expand or get weak, die out or conquered to the man.

Liberals were the "superior in history" to compensate for the misguided, all who came before.

Left: Academia, media, entertainment industry, public school system, government bureaucracies.

All systems are fully entwined with multinational corporate finance and it's oligarchical elite.

Taught to live their bliss, in the moment. That masculinity was evil/outdated vs. the "superior" feminine.

EPILOGUE

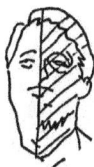

Permitting this mass immigration is the worst kind of treason.

The founders: Only "persons of good character" let in--and no one thought diversity was a strength.

My ancestors built this place you're taking over and they believed it would remain European forever.

Demography is destiny and if you ignore it's effects you and your children will have no destiny.

Mass immigration brings alienation, loss of identity and culture; loss of family values/discord.

Islam exhibits absolute intolerance against dissidents and promotes inhumane punishments.

European women are systematically discriminated, oppressed, molested but you don't hear about it.

They didn't even have these crimes in Europe until the mass immigration started, there was refinement.

Author's Note: Equality is a dangerous myth.

I believe in God's timing so was the book really delayed a year? No, it's the exact day and hour.

While they accomplished one thing after another, you waited patiently to produce something great.

Libs don't want people around with reason/evidence on their side as it causes emotional freakouts.

If he has out-group preferences the home is a mess.

EPILOGUE

HARD LEFT IN EDUCATION

Any teachers who are left are survivors of the hard-left indoctrination environment and the worst.

The replacement of facts and analysis with political hysteria and abuse: that's the public schools.

They don't want diversity at all, they only want a fascism of feelings. Stefan Molyneux

Politics: Not facts but people controlling hysteria by lashing out at opponents in America.

Intergenerational sex (pederasty) is bad. Milo said it was good so he's dead.

If your art is political it's ok when they're in control but later the backlash will be harsh and bold.

Getting rid of 60's shows like Mayberry wasn't a rural purge it was a white purge: now it's city sludge.

NEEDING FLATTERY IS A WEAKNESS

Being open to their flattery is a serious weakness so you'd better get tough or it's over for us.

Do not greet nor receive false teachers into your house or you participate in their evil deeds. John 2

They wanna punish the whole country cuza what some lunatic did--that's the kids.

This generation is so off-base it's a turkey shoot, a cakewalk to correct their fallacy with your talk.

It's like an evil tidal wave as false doctrine (one-ism) takes over everything but it's a lie: nothing.

I was a terrible filthy sinner but God turned it all around, forgot it all and made me a real winner.

EPILOGUE

Each of the 30,000 Christian denominations say they are the only way but it's just Jesus I say.

Satan exists to steal, kill and destroy. How does he do this? Through false doctrines minimizing this guy.

The bible raises man up from slavery and degradation, then they become useful citizens again.

A sermon is only based on the fruit it bares, so ignore all those golden-tongued orators.

Bible tries to get man to face his sins and repent for them, because Jesus' sacrifice *erased* them.

MANY WORDS BRANDS FALSE DOCTRINE

Many words--volubleness or loquacity--marks the false doctrine. Truth may be said in few words quickly.

Look at the *fruits* of religion: we were rich and influential when we were a Christian nation.

The youth don't know, so they pump em full of garbage trying to destroy their mind/keep em below.

If a man walked into a lady's bathroom he woulda been crushed by real men angry/furious too.

Your teachers don't have a clue.

Christians differ on things like baptism etc. But they all agree He died for you/me--that was America.

Everything has it's meaning and identity in Him, He created the universe and everything therein.

God has chosen the foolishness of preaching to save them that believe so He sets them apart, see?

EPILOGUE

If you're a preacher God has anointed you already but what happens when the crowd gets angry?

Saying some crazy hippy spouting lies is your guardian angel? This is crazy and unbelievable!

Churches have fallen into lies, fables and disrepute! It's all from carnality, compromise/no fruits.

SERVING A SMALL GOD

Seems you serve a small God not big One, and you accept other religions as equal = mockery and sin.

Yes! We divide because we hate sin and everything else that HE hates, as he instructs us each day.

It's happened to boys/girls: turned from Jesus to ignorance, paganism and darkness of that world.

People seek joy through religions of works, not realizing it was already done at the cross first.

At war with relatives and maniacs: All over the world they're turning from the truth of God to a lie.

Glib talk but inside rot, perversion and destruction--a buffoon and fraud and you knew it not?

Hah--a man who worshipped his own mind, and his brain! He'll be mowed down like the grass I say.

There are laws so there must be a lawgiver.

Hell is at the end of a Christ-rejecting life.

A false preacher says nothing about the cross--nothing! Also not sin or it's remedy, how wanting.

Man's problem is not lack of intellect but a fallen nature--his heart--which "niceness" covers in part.

EPILOGUE

False healers think they can educate you out of problems, never mentioning sin and the fallen.

Education is not the answer, only salvation is the answer and that comes from a Person.

College professors going to hell talking like that--like Savior means nothing or occult is a good thing.

My pain is greater than I can bare said the sinner.

ENTIRE CONGREGATIONS OF HERESY

Entire congregations go apostate preaching liberalism like pro-sodomite or pro-abortion!

You only care about trendy things cuz you're part of this world and it's unlimited debaucheries.

If your church is that way it's not God but man-made--get out, escape and let Jesus save the day.

The violent hatred towards Christianity is growing daily so preach it I say.

He felt bad about what he did but not enough that Godly sorrow would worketh repentance.

Cunning sinners are always caught, no matter.

Do you worship people--status or stars? Watch as the worms eat them and they disappear.

Even his nation's worst enemies hated him for treacherously selling out his own country.

They're gonna false flag it and blame it on us--that's what they do and we all know it.

Staged terror is part of our vernacular cuz we made it popular as truth-lovers.

EPILOGUE

If we can no longer debate and present our sides then it's tyranny and violence besides.

It's no longer easy preaching the bible as the final authority cuz they think THEY are the authority.

IN PRISON FOR HATE SPEECH

They're hauling pastors off to prison for hate speech, for not bowing to government to deceive.

The left is successful at making simple facts seem rude, evil and unkind.

Gun control persists: Enlarging the state and disempowering citizens is in the left's best interests.

Mexico bans guns and has the highest crime rate in the world.

They yell "do something--not one more child". Not a word about Islamacists killing millions--why?

To prevent mass killings stop drugging our young boys. Alex Jones

A fetus is sentient, feminists!

Trannies degrade our fighting capabilities and make war in the barracks. Any idiot can see this.

Whenever someone says "don't judge" it's them judging YOU. Don't EVER be talked down to!

Judge: Make your own determination of reality, not adapt to "superiors" who censure but are petty.

The "don't judge" myth is either public schools or false religion so judge and don't be chicken.

Psalms starts out with hicks trying to bring down kings. They assemble to plan their evil stings.

EPILOGUE

Mexico: Total gun ban for citizens, highest crime rate in the world yet you go along with this?

Be merciful to me O God, for man would trample or devour me: all day long he oppresses me. Psalms 56: 1

"Be liberal, let us take over, we'll be sweet" then they conquer and kill and they're the same still.

Not born that way: Women are dumbed cuz they want each other's approval more than truth, ok?

COLLUSIONS AGAINST GOD'S PEOPLE

They lie in wait for me/would swallow me up or trample me all day long, and there are many. Psalm 56: 2

Is Trump out of joint? The constitution remains the same no matter who's in power--that's the point.

How the sexes get along is the basis for society but now "he" can beat her up in wrestling, really?

We're now required to lie about biology/punished if we don't. Reason's gone/hearts of stone.

Soon it will be illegal to even teach biology to accommodate the latest liberal cosmology.

How insane a celebrity's profuse apology for mis-gendering nut jobs in this new pathology.

Ruining a girl's state championship for all the undrugged, unsteroided aspirants who haven't flipped.

If you wanna be a girl or boy, do it: take up violin not wreck a sport for all the other participants.

There is no gender fluidity--there are two biological sexes, dummy.

EPILOGUE

Ban baseball bats, knives, screwdrivers, cars. They're used in crimes too so change all the laws.

It's Germany in 1933: they confiscated guns, eliminated free speech and censured the media.

Fill people with psychotropic drugs with "mass killing" on the insert then say it's the guns": jerks.

L.A. has become unrecognizable. In reaction white flight escalates as they turn red states blue.

Governments never give you back what they've taken away, so give the left no quarter, ok?

Why would we possibly need AR-15s? Because the enemy has AR-15s, see?

REPROBATE MINDS ARE INCONVENIENT

A reprobate mind is conditioned not to know evil and insists we do things that are inconvenient.

The left is never, ever satisfied. They will take everyone's rights then turn on their own kind.

Once they get rich they want power which is intoxicating. More and more the left is conquering.

The unified religion is Lucifer.

They seek satan after told they'll feel a wonderful strength, energy, lightness and rapture.

The gun agenda is only a tactic in the goal of total control and that is what every good patriot knows.

They probe in little attacks so later when the main attack happens we don't recognize it.

Youth are an army of brainwashed bots who take the latest political correctness and bully us a lot.

EPILOGUE

First they censure then demonize, arrest then kill--and they're cutting off our money and speech still.

Choose your side but we'll win regardless.

Stay level headed, stay strong. Because they're gonna come in to get you or pull you down.

It's our second amendment right. We need better guns than our enemies, invading mobs or armies.

DON'T CAVE TO THE LEFT

Don't budge one inch when it comes to the left. Don't thrown them a bone because it's like theft.

If your enemy has a sword, get a better sword.

Old lady defends against mobs and thugs. Guns are the equalizer and Trump's betraying us.

Women are shallow and stupid cuz they love The View, Joy Behar and are hypnotized by each other.

Voting is more dangerous than guns--what if a million teens voted in a thug?

Women are stupid, shallow and cruel because they listen to Joy Behar, Whoopi and The View.

Women love to assert their authority thru gossiping/networking and how I hate it.

Virtue signaling defined: Taking the politically correct view on a trendy topic to not seem unkind.

Conservative patriotic husbands of liberal wives cannot get thru to them so see that/do not despise.

It's hard to give up on all women but you just about have to do that, they're just too conformed or fat.

EPILOGUE

I love God and hate liberalism so I guess that is my contribution to the failing nation.

Christianity is not a set of rules but God/a Man who saves us from the whole mess or fools.

Occult is in all Disney movies: hexes, incantations, sorcery, spells, curses--also seen in churches.

Tarot, astrology: With all the time you study occult you ignore Jesus--you're not Christian just a nut.

DISNEY: INSTILL OCCULT CURIOSITY

Disney's plan: Instill occult curiosity, elevate animals and dehumanize humans, basically.

Disney's magical world of witchcraft seduced us as kids and now we're paying for it, ya dig?

Fascinated and snagged by tarot cards she also gets bitchy and fallen cuz that's how it works.

The very things they say they hate their movies are full of. They want guns while you've none of.

Our founders gave us a great trust fund--not gold but the right to self-defend.

Wise as a serpent--we're not supposed to be stupid and God doesn't like it.

Book of Job or Book of Joel Osteen?

Mass deception of the end times is unfolding now.

Gun control is always, without exception, followed by storm troopers and a dictatorship.

Their ratings went from super low to in the tank so of course Joy Behar et. al. are walking it all back.

EPILOGUE

Their plan is to weaponize the third world and then use it to reverse-colonize the first world.

How to bring the west down: Celebrate and glamorize the beta male or call him a clown.

It's not a sign of love to go along with their B.S. just because they virtue signal as feminists.

POLITICAL VIEWS TRIGGER TENSION

Not only will they reject you for your political views they'll fire, gossip, ruin, and slander you.

The archetype of the older white Christian family man is racist and it's an insult and false.

History of the 20th century: giving up what worked for what sounded nice.

It is our God-given right to defend ourselves against lunatic mobs invading our house.

The constitution says THIS--it's not up for debate. But the left can't debate anyway, they run away.

Since the conservative deals in rational, logical arguments the left can never win a debate and exits.

The left is so boring and shallow, always virtue signaling on trendy topics based on hell below.

The left's only argument with logic and reason is: I just don't like it so I'll accuse you of racism.

Go ahead and make your art political--you're in the wrong and soon they'll all see it, get me gal?

Go ahead and block, ban, purge and censure: the populist movement will grow beyond measure.

EPILOGUE

Generally we just wanna be left alone but if you keep forcing us to agree there's gonna be fallout, see?

Calvinists start on time they don't wait for the last stragglers dragging in, adapting to decline.

You're so dumb and shallow you'll accept any line to tow but you'll switch just as fast, ya know.

You'll accept any crap (not having your own map) and then virtue-signal to the crowd of cads.

The only way you'd ever see reason is if the other's committed treason to that view, appeasin'.

In a war you recognize the enemy as evil, period. You don't sit and argue his pros and cons, get real!

GLAMORIZED HERESY

Study: All growing churches are conservative, all declining churches are liberal, no exceptions.

They threw away orthodox Christianity and adopted the secularist globalism we call church today.

The whore church like Methodists are losing hundreds of thousands a year: apostates and queers.

The false church never preaches sin and repentance if that goes against the party line perchance.

Theological conservatism is the key to congregational growth, without exception.

Conservative Christians growing and maintaining faith multigenerationally but libs aren't having babies.

They're the voice of the "excluded and marginalized" so the white man was the class to despise.

EPILOGUE

The great mass blowback against political correctness found it's home online.

They want us like Brazil: Guns in hands of cops and criminals while we're caught in the middle.

Your interest in them is tantamount to people-worship so stop it.

Societies are rich because the people there are intelligent with an aptitude to make things work.

Public schools are government schools to sell you the current narrative and thus you're not intelligent.

When thugs invade your house remember to be inclusive and show em where the refrigerator is.

The hated racist is "alienated by the other".

According to Pelosi we oughta thank the Dreamers and the parents cuz they're better than us.

THEY CALL FREE SPEECH RACISM

Watch out for the kids who say free speech is the same as racism. Yes, it's gone that far ma'am.

Watch out for somebody who says they love everybody cuz either they're lying or their crazy.

According to UC saying you're not racist means you're racist—it's a micro-aggression they insist.

The Puritans (which I am) were into austere order and solemnity (no chattering or jocularity).

The Puritans got that way as an adaptation/reaction to the debaucheries of 18th century England.

We've endured treachery, deceit, laxness/laziness so now we're reversing to the other extreme.

EPILOGUE

Our youth are disordered from programming. We're sick of this crap and want a return to reality.

We know the exact signs of liberalism and will respond, in kind, every time but we'll stay refined.

Mega-churches are swinging clubs.

Clinton opposed gay marriage for decades until she hopped on the train to win the progressives.

APPROVAL TRANSCENDS TRUTH

That's the way women are: getting the approval of each other supersedes truth-seeking, wow.

Destroy us by making us lackluster--no culture, not even gender, conformity to the master.

They aren't partisan views, they're get-even views. Alan Dershowitz

Women have never been so well treated as by western men yet you're conflating like they're all hellions.

Feminism has become a joke and high-paid power women are distancing themselves, unyoked.

If your "art" is political you'll be so embarrassed later (eat crow when things change): disfavor.

You've been taught bunk in the schools, ball-faced lies. Do your art around it and be despised.

Don't talk em out of it just let em do themselves in. Evil brings itself down in family or friends.

They're personally unattractive cuz that is giving in to patriarchy but this is deceptive malarkey.

Be a sweet little decent lady from the fifties--now you'll have power, not thru roles or filled with sin.

EPILOGUE

Feminism makes men enemy, wimped and cuckolded or an instant adversary sensing treachery.

Feminists deny hating men but what about ruining the boy scouts? The list goes on, feminism sux.

BOOB JOBS AND CLEAVAGES

A boob job doesn't give you power, many get even bigger boobs and it all goes down from there.

Before the grossification of culture men preferred elegance: tiny boobs, slimness, niceness.

The boobjob dame may also be into occult: tarot cards etc. cuz it all goes together in America.

Men should return to reality and actually feel fear of boob jobs/sex dolls, fake reality not the rose.

She can decide later it was rape and you're toast--destroyed. Get her to sign it or it's best to avoid.

What if three years from now she takes a radical feminist course and decides it was rape?

No need for signs of violence/she can chase him for weeks--his life is still destroyed as she speaks.

The very essence of civilization is that men will sacrifice themselves to save the women.

Left destroys everything attractive in favor of the bland, the mediocre and the dysfunctional.

Political correctness is a war on noticing. Steve Sailer

Gender/women's studies are thinly-veiled leftist propaganda vehicles not academic disciplines.

EPILOGUE

Never argue with the idiots who bring you down to their level and beat you with their "experiences".

Being drawn into heated arguments is fruitless and exhausting so we stand idle and in denial.

Having lost ability to think they can hold two contradictory premises in their head without a blink.

THE LEFT IS LIKE LASTING RUST

Like rust, the radical leftist corrosive presence in our midst never sleeps, so either can we.

If there is no brown in the rainbow it must be racist and corrected (against natural order as God did).

If you don't play by their rules you are quickly and viciously ostracized as stupid bigots and fools.

Everything must change without reason or logic as constantly shifting boundaries destroys societies.

Constantly changing the left keeps us vigilant as to what is acceptable behavior and what is not.

The left keeps it's brutal power thus: by embarrassing and scaring everyone into silence.

Only strict obedience to the anti-logic of the left will do.

We can't dialogue with the left using it's concepts and language lest our own viewpoint changes.

Gender and women's studies based on cultural Marxism are inherently non-academic disciplines.

Communist takeover so hidden under obscure texts or curriculum we just couldn't see em.

EPILOGUE

Communist takeover was shady, hidden under unlikely curriculum titles like "American Studies".

While we snoozed they stole our defensive weaponry--allegiance to the constitution/being free.

Always tell em their war is for "freedom" and "democracy" yet no speech or opinion you see.

WEAPONIZED CLOUDY PHILOSOPHY

Weaponized cloudy philosophy into ideological anthrax ready to deploy at a moment's notice.

Radical environmentalism, artistic communism, psych-analysis of opponents = multiculturalism.

Left came up with "repressive tolerance" (for everyone but us), also known as political correctness.

Embarrassed for sex (that's you later) when you wake up to degradation of public schools, a mess.

Their goal is to shut down speech making us vassals and malleable, fearful of their punishment.

Make us so confused, timid and apprehensive of punishment we become basket cases not patriots.

Boob jobs and tarot cards.

Black Panther will be in school curriculums as reparations teaching white children what they ruined.

Panther raises black self esteem but also pathological sense of grievance against white people.

They've been given an attractive myth as honorary citizens of Wakanda not oppressed in America.

EPILOGUE

As they have fantasies of power and success we are to feel shame and guilt for creating that mess.

We are to feel shame and guilt for the deeds our ancestors actually accomplished--think of that.

What's making you sick: victim ideology politics.

History is there to take us off the train tracks of ignorant inevitability and restore our will freely.

Trump's gonna decriminalize pot: reining in Sessions and making him hot!

LOVING LEFT LOVES WAR

The loving left is always calling for WAR, in a reversal like we've never seen from long before.

Feminists letting themselves go because to look good would please men-- patriarchy--their foe.

Feminists accept their fat because they have a right to be anything they want even that.

Are men really catcalling these unattractive, fat, mannish harridans, the feminists? Oh come on....

Men used to catcall sweet young ladies and it was flattering but now it's called "disempowering".

How funny a fat harridan complaining about catcalling--the feminists are falsely accusing!

Why should they take a bath, why should they do anything? Pleasing to men? that would be giving in.

Why should she lose weight for him? She'll gain more and end up alone or with cats she adores.

Majority of American females wanna create a home for husband and kids, anathema to feminists.

EPILOGUE

New feminists look like they smell, and smell like they look but with sweet little ladies it's all it took.

Old feminists purposely look like old hags with blue hair. A lady is pleasing at any age, not a scare.

Her new feminist friends will be a dark spirit invading the household and you'll feel the cold.

Worse thing is: sick feminists know nothing about politics but get in their licks and have influence.

NEW FEMINISM: JUST BE RICH

The new feminist wants to be "famous and rich, not A crazy bitch" because it's divisive/leftist.

Let the feminist in and soon you'll see tarot cards, Harry Potter books even lesbian stuff--yuk!

Feminists are not for women but getting attention and mimicking all they hear from vermin.

Absent father, dominant mother = Jezebel spirit: don't bother.

A man can only love a woman if he respects her so stop demanding it and act right for it.

How can he respect you if you follow the feminist crowd of fats, acting like that, spewing crap?

Ha ha you complaining about male cat calls--are you kidding, you expect us to believe you all?

A woman who looks nice for a man (dressing for him) is a "sell out, man"--that's the feminist scam.

The California bay area liberal elite groupthink wants to ban the holy bible and make it illegal.

EPILOGUE

In this deep state mess, espionage is a science, propaganda an art and sabotage is a business.

Libtards think gun free zones stop mass shootings--nothing proves more they're a mental illness.

Tyrants in history felt invincible but when people woke up they were thrown into graves, humbled.

It's not sensitivity over truth it's moral posturing about sensitivity over truth. Jordan Peterson

MODERN ART GOES TO HELL

Modern art: edgy but empty

Before putting too-edgy "art" out there ask yourself: would grandma approve? Modern is uncouth.

Through your art you sow seeds of discord and that's how society's are taken down by hordes.

Encroaching artistic fascism of left: only body fluids and self-humiliation remains fair game.

Europeans are being asked to replace the beauty of the past with the brutality of the present.

Why beauty (the profound/remarkable) matters: without it life's in tatters, there are no answers.

Encroaching artistic fascism of left: only body fluids and self-humiliation remains fair game.

Just as Puritans were a reaction to filth and debauchery we too became decent, cautious, leery

Beauty and art is aspirational: it sparks the human spirit to go even higher than we're capable.

EPILOGUE

There **ARE** objective beauty standards and it's not a piece of trash in a gallery, it's all backwards.

Beauty is a universal human need elevating the human spirit not ugly buildings as we now have it.

Now we just have nihilism, meaninglessness and unhappiness all reflected in our surroundings.

Surrounded by ugliness we are degraded in our spirit as it drains away capacity for happiness.

The replacement with crap for everything that was wonderful is horrifying to sensitive people.

All "art" is filtered through identity politics before gallery acceptance.

THE UGLY IS BEAUTIFUL WE'RE TOLD

Due to identity politics they shame us into thinking the ugly is beautiful or the hideous is suitable.

Beauty and order reflects heaven and paradise, ugly disorder reflects hell like the hoarders.

Modern art: obscurantism pushed in pretentious flowery language shaming people to gush over it.

If you don't "jive and resonate" with this crap you're called "uncultured and ignorant" about art.

Are you really serious about this modern art, trying to find the profound and deep meaning? HAH

Laughing artists never had to study anatomy but can just spatter paint and rake in their money.

Artists are the "sophisticates" who self-delude that it all has meaning to them, the superior beings.

EPILOGUE

We see trash as trash, but the elevated artist see's the deeper meaning from higher intelligence.

It's all a joke but if they can ascribe meaning to it with pretentious language, they won't go broke.

Dance should stand on it's own, not be encased in pretentious words and meaningless concepts.

Elitism and obscurantism go together: if you can make sense of nothing you're elite or "whatever".

WHEN ART IS OBSCURE

When art has no objective meaning or beauty they rely on obscurantism to dress it up: creepy.

Sometimes their "art" descriptions are three pages long of pure BS and obscurantism, no kiddin'.

Can they let their ridiculous/meaningless art stand on it's own? No, they dress it up, then "oh!"

Trash with a three page description of how meaningful it is and they always get away with it.

If you point out how art is crap despite pretentious words of the hour you're censured and fired.

The elevation of the mediocre to the pinnacle of achievement pulls down the pinnacle in a minute.

To destroy Shakespeare liberals simply elevated crap and then everything fell into their lap.

Everything traditional like Shakespeare is now being redressed with a "hip twist" which sux.

Art should require talent and skill, not this modern stuff, it's swill.

EPILOGUE

Pretentious obscurantism surrounding crap art: They do this every time and it's the phoniest part.

If it offends the politically correct it's not art?

You must pass the ideologically purity test to be seen as avant-garde in the modern art world.

Art must reflect the narrative or you're punished as "abusive".

Modern art has become the strange mix of the hyper-real while being utterly devoid of content.

MODERN ART IS WEAPONIZED

Modern art has become weaponized cuz they control the narrative or overthrow reality instead.

They control the narrative so don't get sucked into premise upon which their "art" is presented.

Modern art closes us from the transcendent while capturing our soul by the cheesy way presented.

The transcendent is beauty and all else degrees of ugliness but we were decent/orderly nevertheless.

All thru history it was conservative forces that built civilization and liberals tearing it down.

We should view modern art as a reflection of the final phase of civilization.

Transcendent beauty allows the soul of the viewer to interface with the greater spiritual realm.

True art raises moral consciousness while organizing understanding of what is healthy/unhealthy.

Poli-subversive art specifically attacks institutions or civic ideas elevating the west above others.

EPILOGUE

Modern art undermines the philosophical system of an entire group, it's beliefs, customs and values.

Modern art is designed to destroy our historical narrative and the BEAUTY of our spiritual identity.

Modern art uses antithetical elements to disrupt our sense of awe, self-recognition and beauty.

MODERN ART IS A MORAL VACUUM

Modern art opens up a moral vacuum where all is meaningless: weaponized against it's own.

Modern art simply politicized anti-art masquerading as virtuous art with genocide it's only arbiter.

Modern art is smelly reality not depth, yet with pseudo-intellectual notes they justify this filth.

Shock art blocks our relation to the transcendent (beauty), we can't relate to ourselves and it's empty.

Protest culture is infiltrating all schools as we see mass walkouts and teachers too think they're cool.

You're not artsy if you're edgy, that's the cheap way. True artists create beauty and love decency.

So you're artistic if you adapt to the peanut gallery's debauchery? That's not audacity just nasty.

I didn't think you were that cheap but now I see it's all you peeps: evil offshoots off the main tree.

I had no idea you were this cheap, evident hater of good, lowdown, cheesy/subversive of decency.

Political art is always subversive of traditions of decency and goodness so how could you trust this?

EPILOGUE

Stand up comedy's become repetitive cuz it's the same groups targeted--this isn't "edginess".

Artists are petrified of going outa the prescribed boundaries of correctness, producing lousiness.

CAN'T EVEN SAY IT'S INTERESTING

No one says anything interesting cuz it may taint their careers and boy are they a bunch of bores.

A true avant-garde artist is just himself not a liberal fascist.

Society is degenerating, mental illness is exploding and people don't know God, their Champion.

We've been domesticated and made weak, our families broken up, men and women shallow and dumb.

Identity politics defined: Vote for someone who looks like you, it's easier than thinking too.

When teachers tell kids to walk out it's not "spontaneous uprising" but rather their own agenda/lying.

So if I don't agree with your gun-grabbing agenda I don't care about kids? Watch this sly fib by libs.

The kids refuse to sit in classrooms with armed teachers, they want to punish us all in the suburbs.

They say all masculinity is bad, oppressing women--not that we need men to keep out the vermin.

Identity politics is a terrible thing, setting us against each other--it's Satan not our Christian brothers.

Identity politics is pure tribalism and playing that game is murderous like with white Africans.

EPILOGUE

Learn to proceed despite your "victimization status" and be normal everyday chumps like us.

Old white males are the main targets however they are given the lowest victimization status.

Virtue signaling is being politically correct to get approval and an immature trait needing removal.

DIVERSITY is *NOT* OUR STRENGTH

The Lord has fixed all the borders of the earth (divisions of land, sea and nations). Psalm 74: 17

We haven't lost our homeland--we're still here--but we may as well have, living in dread and fear.

Any mention of "race" and it's like a hot stove--they want everyone the same, kept below.

The churches are pushing melting pot integration thinking it will end racism and it's falsehood ma'am.

The churches want us all brown when God made us all different--this is falsehood again.

Mass immigration is underhandedly clever: the left found a way to attain power and hold it forever.

Multiculturalism means we all die together. Katie Hopkins

The major narrative: Whites are always the oppressors and nonwhites are always victims for sure.

Liberalism: absolutely every racial difference is due to racism not inborn so continue to let em in.

Globalists are anti-human: make us hate ourselves, attack family, ruin culture, centralize government.

Globalist Gameplan: establish new societies that lack identity--culture, race, gender, you and me.

EPILOGUE

How would you like millions of strangers coming over your border? It's what's happening all over.

Shoved aside in own family cuz you're white while they put up a stranger who married in tight.

PESSIMISTIC ART OF DECADENCE

Age of Decadence: Defensiveness, pessimism, materialism, frivolity, no God, welfare, foreigners.

Great numbers of foreigners arrive at the end of empire weakening as old grievances are aired.

Border control still: the Obama hold-overs are incompetent, corrupt, and anti-law enforcement.

Africa: where obdurate tribalism trumps political persuasion and envy carries the day.

It's not that i don't wanna be with you, I just wanna be alone. KK motto

The northern Europeans have strong out-group favoring which becomes toxic/self-annihilating.

Reason for deficit debt today: providing first world services to third world pops who can't pay.

Having a strong in-group identity they're happy to use violence at the slightest resistance.

Be the immune response to the multicultural cancer destroying/eating away our countries.

Secularization is globalism but nationalist is Christian.

The west is the best and the reason everyone wants to come here is because of that. Gavin McInnes

France was always socialist and way left, look at the result: a migrant flood but still they're stuck.

EPILOGUE

My new picturestrip is **OPEN BORDER:** not that we want it but we have it and it's wreaking havoc.

It seems like a quiet neighborhood but in an instant things could change and they're all deranged.

WHEN THE HEDGE IS DOWN

The minute your walls are down inflows evil all around even though they seemed so quiet ya' know.

A known Marxist, completely false pope.

Pope: Open your borders, world government is good, need a world gov church, the family is bad.

Highest murder rate/stabbings and muggings: London is incredibly dangerous and frightening.

Come on in--as long as you don't stay, come el norte.

Trump ratings up not just about money but confronting global tyranny and the invasion by our enemy.

World is speedily realigning to Christian nationalist lines after globalist secularism and all it's crimes.

Export secular modernity in the form of globalized human/reproductive rights creating blight.

Things taken as a hallmark of decline and decadence are now seen as rights reflecting human progress.

Globalism driven by devices such as "disembedding" cultures or "detraditionalization" like vultures.

Traditional moral values are replaced by "life style values" where anything else goes too.

According to the left, Americans should be sickened and ashamed of the world's greatest nation.

EPILOGUE

All their sitcoms are of urban America, they care nothing for us country folk fearing things like Sharia.

We have two distinct cultures here: the urbanized liberal globalist vs the traditionalist heartland.

GLOBALIST TRENDIES

Globalist trendies care nothing for the rural, the permanent, the traditional with Christian roots.

Disembedding: The globalist device replacing traditions and cultures with secular lifestyles.

Translocal consumer based lifestyle values replaced the traditional events we went to.

In the face of threat to a sense of place/identity/security people tend to re-assert religious markers.

The re-assertion of tradition is a mechanism of resistance against secular globalization/what fun.

They can't protect global business while also protecting local customs, religions and traditions.

The liberal globalist pope disappoints at every turn.

Prison: being locked in with em. That's how many learned about borders and the necessity of fencin'.

Putin keeps the western church out: not just seen as secular but pagan, and I see his point here.

Russia sees us as reviving abortion (child sacrifice), and pagan marriages through gay rights.

Russia sees us as reviving witchcraft--think Harry Potter and also England, an invasion catastrophe.

EPILOGUE

The irony is: the vacuum feminism created has made women the victims of aggressive males.

A culture of weak men doesn't result in strong women, but unprotected women. Steven Turley

The battered wife of a feeble continent.

If we're gonna be a minority in our own country, what was it all for?

AGEISM AND GLOBALISM

Ageism/Brexit: Forward-looking youth felt betrayed and victimized by elderly wanting to leave.

White flight = downward spiral of ghettoization.

If "everyone's the same" disparate outcomes "must" be due to immorality like racism or slavery.

Koran encourages taking enemy women as sex slaves and also children so of course men love it.

Only 7% of Germans Nazis but look at the bedlam/lives lost. Same with Islam, it only takes less.

PEOPLE PROBLEMS

A life's work: creativity coming through learned skills and you're ready to show/what a thrill.

The more you relax the more you'll work. Leisure is the key for all great geniuses for sure.

Yours is the type of intricate/delicate work that requires all day leisure after producing this treasure.

If you can't explain it simply, you don't understand it well enough. Albert Einstein

So you went off a cliff, so what. All great geniuses had quirks and ruts.

EPILOGUE

Recognize patterns in human relationships and you've got it--a happy life managing the peeps.

Don't blame them for their lunacy, they've been programmed to act that way but are still guilty.

My only reality is the crow in the morning and crickets at night: stay here now, you'll stay high.

You can be shining bright as high as a kite but God removes charisma and you're a blight.

NEVER FEAR WHEN WICKED PROSPER

Never fear when the wicked prosper because soon they're mowed down-- jokers and paupers.

An inheritance hastily gotten will come to nothing or unblessed in the end.

Be careful cuz everything can change in a minute. Great loss is the best teacher then build back up.

Stay close to God and He'll show you who they are cuz evil spirits block/you won't be a star.

What you visualize seeks you but unless you're sick of what lies behind it won't ever find you.

If you think you're special/get things done they call it narcissistic but I call that dream-killin'.

Think of life as a road to eternity. Repentance is the journey that proves you're worthy, not modernity.

God said He'd bless the work of your hands so work then wait for everything to come/rake it in.

He never blessed jokers, they were minions who will now be mowed down while you make millions.

EPILOGUE

Do not say "Why were the old days better than these?" For it is not wise that you ask this. Eccl 7:10

Fools and fanatics are certain of themselves while the wise are full of doubts. Bertrand Russell

GET INTELLIGENT KIDS IN *ORDER*

Wait until you *want* to work, that's the trick. Never get tense to achieve, fools force the fit.

The best thing you can do for your child is providing work space and teach em to keep order.

When success equals life and failure equals death, you're in trouble. Let God increase you, double.

Men tend to be undone thru lust, women thru vanity. Stefan Molyneux

We must accept the difference in brain size, IQ and neuroconnections--see it, or destruction.

Bye bye cutie, it has to do with IQ of me and you.

There is a universally preferable behavior: a rational group of secular ethics. Stefan Molyneux

We all have to live with the less intelligent while before they were restrained by God--not now.

Stop expecting intelligent stuff from less intelligent people. Stefan Molyneux

Obesity and poverty result from low IQ since deferred gratification increases with intelligence.

Idiots think they're geniuses and geniuses are humble: that's the Dunning-Kruger Effect on people.

"You're overthinking this" said the monkey to the human or to her by her loving manipulators.

EPILOGUE

IF SURROUNDED BY VIOLENT MORONS

If surrounded by monkeys threatened by your intellectual capacity then my advice is: stay away.

The natural curb to our appetite is consequences. Stefan Molyneux

What makes you smart is knowing you're mostly an idiot--opposite to the Dunning-Kruger Effect.

It's outrageous and outlandish and you know it/can't stop it.

Do not be quick to be angry or vexed, for anger and vexation lodge in the bosom of fools. Eccl 7: 9

His two sides--the disparity--was so great that to hold em both in my head I just denied the other.

Hate to tell you this but virtue signaling on trendy topics is not being an "artist"

The bible says not to depend on future windfalls, just enjoy each day as God designed for y'all.

Wife of the alcoholic goes insane due to the spirit in him and pathological devices to maintain.

Wife of alcoholic feels to blame and gets sicker than he ever could in codependency with the lame.

True glamour is just being yourself and not conforming to anyone but God and that's being decent.

The feeling of going beyond a problem, the joy of completed work done, nothing tracking me hon'.

Just face it: You are the best at what you do, no one can do it like you and that's all you gotta know.

In order to get this well you had to get that sick. It was a low bottom that inverted to the best/that's it.

EPILOGUE

In order to get this good you had to go lower than others for some reason and it's embarrassing.

It's a matter of duplicity--him portraying one fella but then there's another and it's filled with hell.

The best saints were the worst sinners.

ENANTIODROMIA: CONVERTING TO OPPOSITES

Enantiodromia: Everything converting to it's opposite. Worst sinners become best saints/legit.

Relax, let the rest take care of itself. There's an impetus to completion that happens in spite of self.

You shouldn't have to explain why. If they don't get it on their own it's begone, later, ciao, goodbye.

You shouldn't have to explain why you wanna be alone in solitude/you don't know for how long.

Avoid and ignore all social pulls. The kind making you feel guilty for it's all of your life it dulls.

It's not that I don't wanna be with you but I wanna be by myself more.

I think of Carol who never called back, she had class.

What is retirement if not release from all social expectations as well as anything else/obstructions?

I don't want anyone to expect anything from me or pressure me in any way/a genius blocker/not ok.

You must now eliminate all anti-genius forces.

Avoid and ignore all social pulls. The kind making you feel guilty for it's all a bunch of bull.

EPILOGUE

An event happens and you won't even remember it. Forget events/go eternal: rise above all this.

Inside is a phantasmagoria of delight, all from rejecting the outer world of terror, sadness & blight.

You're too accessible.

VICTORY RESTS WITH THE LORD

The horse is made ready for the day of battle but victory rests with the Lord. Proverbs 21: 31

A gossip betrays a confidence, so avoid a man who talks too much.   Proverbs 20: 19

In respect of the doc he won't underline but the bible is to increase understanding, mark it up!

Loss of respect for inferiors is the necessary step to your life's work.

Around a gossip you feel like a leaking boat--no control (over what people know) and down you go.

Public reputation is very important and the gossip holds the cards. Women relish this power/it's hard.

Men gossip too but it's like a female art perfected to a "T" as she balances forces like you and me.

Too many things I couldn't reconcile. It's too much disparity between her acts and "nice" style.

Shame puts you at a lower level looking "up to" them. Jesus doesn't want that so now shame's gone.

What's gone? Sting of shame, white as snow. With Jesus that's something you gotta know.

Don't worry you were hidden. Under God's wings you're protected and they have no recollection.

EPILOGUE

Good homemaking is: keeping stuff out.

Traumatized people act insane, you acted insane because you were traumatized, leave it at that.

ADDICTION AND LOST TALENTS

Addicted to whatever, the frontal (moral) dwindled and you lost all morality and style [clever].

Just one slight change cuz you hit on the right thing and bingo everything reassembles, done.

Scared of her dark soul: She was cold as hell but such a deceptively nice outer shell I couldn't tell.

He talks beautifully but says nothing.

Get up too late and you make mistakes.

Since the best talents ripen late they call you a has-been who never-was on the way up, but wait.

An ancestor had disparate views from the village so they tied her up to the dock/later she drowned.

I felt like a leaky boat you gossiping like that.

We have fond memories but things have changed, don't hold on lest it all derange like in a cage.

If you live in mud you'll be filled with mud. Watch your words/how you think in liberal crud.

When I asked "what should I do" the Lord said "do what is front of you".

I have desire for order and evident cerebrotonia: fear of disorder, the Puritan reaction to fear.

What's the rush? You can accomplish more by doing nothing much.
Do nothing then the angels finish it anyway.

EPILOGUE

By doing nothing you are accomplishing so much more--the brain can roam, untracked from the bore.

Allow nothing in that tracks the brain. Keep it nimble to God's instructions, let Him have the reins.

Have only in-group preferences and you'll see your life light up.

You keep going back to teaching videos but can't take so much of that ya know, shift modes.

As you shift from OUT to IN, the world will resist cuz it wants your "yes" but it's too much a mix.

His/her success doesn't take anything from you, ok?

PUT PRIVACY FIRST

Only way you can be mindful of privacy invasion is needing it yourself. The others, not on your life.

Facebook: Get offa that thing cuz it's only a small slice of reality and it's blocking you, truly.

How to get high: come into total order.

Put a wall around your home but also around your past with a sign "no fishing"--leave it alone.

After a lifetime of unpaid effort and striving without thriving someone discovers you: new life.

It happens suddenly, remember that. Always be ready, hat and packed.

It's gonna happen suddenly so stay packed/hold onto your hat, you're whole and that's that

Don't go out before you're ready and be patient. Avoid public opprobrium and embarrassment.

EPILOGUE

Let Creative Act develop as it should like doing a puzzle. Not a bunch of projects to bamboozle.

Many useless projects quickly accomplished and that's it--give me a break. It's a lifetime/must wait.

Talents are genetic but also the form of symptoms rolling out should you fall, like getting frenetic.

THE DRY YEARS WEREN'T LOST TIME

You didn't lose any time cuz you had to take that detour to learn the lessons and become refined.

Videos track your precious mind, music evokes thought. Severely limit internet and you'll be hot.

Computer fatigue makes me tired but music brings me back, instantly in fact.

Chattering is talking too much, cackling is jocularity: silly laughter, hysteria cracking on a fire.

People waste time self-entertaining but creativity is the highest way of being.

Just wait quietly on the periphery until YOUR TIME has come, which it will cuz God promised us.

Take your eyes off people cuz they can't help you only God hears and knows to send angels soon.

You've been programmed all your life and thus you're a bore. Now open to God/the true self more.

The most fertile times are doing nothing.

Nothing done yet nothing undone it all just happens.

Don't worry if few enjoy your work or don't like it. WAIT for that ONE for success/who'll map it.

EPILOGUE

The angels don't care where you've been, they just see the steps of your progression, applaudin'.

In a Great Work the audience is narrow so God'll have to take care of it (discovered by accident).

Get your mind off of him/her. They're just people and will be gone. Focus on your champion, God.

FALLEN NATURE OF MAN

When a fallen/rebellious nature has claimed it's place in our souls we suffer from his sin ya know.

Painfree: Withdraw your emotions from the situation and see it as a social scientist or therapist.

Don't worry cuz the solution is within you. Just see it and the game plan rolls out, predestined too.

To rid obstruction (him) just listen to your obstruction-remover, God from the beginning.

Never preach "self-love" unless you also preach repentance cuz without it you can't love yourself.

I aspire to the highest not feel hopeless--the difference between poetry and porn I guess.

I'm either in bliss with God's kiss cuz He thinks I'm adorable or in the pit of hell and life is horrible.

But man, with all his honor and pomp, does not remain: he is like the beasts that perish. Psalm 49:12

Like the wolf who starves/dies after rejection from the pack, ostracism kills. Love God for He fills the bill.

The immature are always virtue signaling on trendy topics and we're sick of it.

EPILOGUE

How to get work done: take the day off. It works every time and it's more fun/not under the gun.

Human life is solitary, poor, nasty, brutish and short. Thomas Hobbes

My home is my castle and if you make me leave you are my worst enemy and what a hassle.

YOUR HOME IS PARADISE!

Home: paradise, climate and people control. Outside gates: hell, chaos and omnipresent chemicals.

I went to your boring potluck to please you and now you're bugging me again/not social like you!

I'll go to a prayer study if you finally start on time and not wait for stragglers to walk in/draw that line.

I'm not going to your parties anymore to be bored, targeted or embarrassed in public and that is IT.

No, I'm not going to your party to see you virtue signal, get attention or gush/bash like millennials.

Don't start your meeting when the last straggler walks in--enforce some discipline, hell with em.

Work your butt off and create something. Not flap your mouth to get attention, but nothing.

Success doesn't come from facebook, the east or west but from God who puts you up as best.

I planted the seed but for harvest I gotta wait, with God I have date.

We'll come out of happy isolation when we're ready and not before, not having to explain it either.

Give her the fruit of her hands, and let her own works praise her in the gates of the city. Phil. 4:8

EPILOGUE

The bread of idleness is: gossip, discontent and self-pity like we see in that mean old bitty.

THE HUSBAND TRUSTS HER IN CONFIDENCE

The heart of her husband trusts in her confidently and relies on and believes in her securely. Prov 31: 11

You should never apologize for just wanting to be alone or as a couple excluding all but your throne.

Every prudent man acts out of knowledge, but a fool exposes his folly. Prov. 13: 16

What a revelation: I have a right to never be seen, never go anywhere or never answer the phone.

The only people who understand me are my housekeeper, my husband and my dog but I'm not odd.

Of course it's not overnight success because you're unknown and waiting to be discovered.

Chaos, starts to take shape, perfects itself.

Anyone who says "there are many paths" is of the antichrist and stinks--needs a spiritual bath.

You are so great without all that--you don't need to sink into swill to get attention you dingbat.

You are bringing opprobrium to your ancestors who are sick with disgust as you've broken their trust.

Satan will beat you to death with your past sins until learning the secret of victory: Christ died for me.

Like a gold ring in a pig's snout is a beautiful woman who shows no discretion. Prov. 11: 22

EPILOGUE

Don't let their debauched spirit get on you or you'll find yourself doing and saying bad things too.

Nothing--you talk about nothing and I'm supposed to answer your phoning or let you in honey?

Don't interrupt enemy (by showing their fallacy) while they're making a huge mistake in front of me.

I died but God brought me back with a Creative Act. As tunnel went black I called to Jesus in fact.

Relax, you're really good in fact the best so just wait and fast.

She comforts, encourages, and does him only good as long as there is life within her. Prov 31: 12.

WICKEDNESS WON'T ESTABLISH

A man cannot be established through wickedness, but the righteous cannot be uprooted. Prov 12: 3

Don't ever work with people who don't share your work ethic because it bring disgust and I mean it.

SIN: He hides, plans evil, covers tracks and you're always surprised cuz you thought he was back.

{Just wait and see:} Good men act from knowledge but fools expose their folly. Proverbs 13: 16

A wise son heeds his father's instruction but a mocker does not listen to rebuke. Prov. 13: 1

It's not that I don't wanna see you/them it's that I wanna be alone--that's two separate things.

You have every right to be alone so get that thru your head. Never explain solitude needs, I said.

EPILOGUE

New videos line up on right then all Christian restraint takes a flight and you're a fallen knight.

On a scale of 1 to 10 they're a one (nothin') and you're a ten cuz you work all day and get 'er dun.

He who walks with the wise grows wise, but a companion of fools suffers harm. Proverbs 13: 8.

Why should you adapt to them? It's an insult, think about that and firmly stand your ground.

Finally you stop tracking em cuz you see how irrelevant and besides people aren't the same again.

The hand of the diligent rules and the lazy sluggard is a fool.

It's hard work but nothing you can force cuz it's creative of course.

We all have our sins and that's one of them, a common one in men.

Deadlines are creative-blockers so release the deadline then finish it all up like famous rockers.

YOU MUST KNOW YOU'RE BEST

You know you're the best cuz you've worked all your life and it's daily diligence not self-disgust.

You're a hard worker but on the wrong thing: false, for approval, debauched or virtue signaling.

Jesus erased what happened when possessed with the devil and washes clean of remorse, so awful.

You found your correct groove--your cats and dogs just want music so just do that, I behoove.

It's all personality coming through and that's what it's all about with them discovering you.

EPILOGUE

You were supposed to go through all that so forget when it fell flat or you fell flat on your back.

For total freedom to be yourself just be nice.

Just protect me from the world so I can work.
Low IQ/weakness: less restraint--the dumb or weak become indecent.

My work surge shows how much it hurt to be misunderstood.

Just be exceptional, hard-working, inventive and good.

It's copy, that's all. That's more than you can say, a bore.

THE WORDMAN DESERVES HIS WAGES

After all this creativity you deserve something.

It doesn't have to make sense. You just did it.

Yah I went wrong, who didn't, it was the age.

How dare you come in like that bringing down the tone.

Varmints: just her way of worming into the household darnit.

They know exactly nothing and just wanna hangout. Don't let it be your house, you're not a pitstop.

I can understand Michael needing three doors--that's how far to be a star.

It's not that I don't want to see you it's that I want to be alone, not see anyone, nothing etched in stone.

Who gains most respect: he who isn't hanging around.

He with most going on must have less going on around.

You wanna come to mind not blow your horn.

EPILOGUE

What a revelation: I have a right to never be seen, never go anywhere or never answer the phone.

Not fame, just money and privacy.

Nothing you can fake, just be yourself.

Insane when captured by projections of another—an eclipsed personality is mental disorder.

Nothing you can fake, can't force the fit = suddenly you're it.

Wives, provide structure for your man. He needs guidance and to direct his brain, then he can.

YOUR UNIQUE MAGNETIC FORCE

They will know you by your extremely unique magnetic force so I say again, just be yourself.

Why'd she say that? And when I told him, why did he say things sizing her up? Confusion, huh.

Once you grasp the impact of wrong words you choose carefully of course.

Lower self: grudges, resentments, jealousies. Higher self: clarity, forgiveness, new life, discoveries.

Family of origin issues = mate selection of alcoholic wifebeater.

When God's done with me I'm done with this place. Charles Lawson

Gospel is a person. You receive Him you're saved, you reject Him you're lost— no creed, it's Christ.

Don't stake your soul for eternity over ignorance of God's word, a common tragedy.

About bible issues they're as ignorant as they can be, with only superficial tidbits and mockery.

EPILOGUE

Hidden sinner is always working it in his reprobate mind: Steal, embezzle, kill but seem kind.

He who covers his sins will not prosper. Proverbs 28:13

If to live is Christ and to die is gain, what can they do to a man like that?

Christ cried, a man of men.

It's not about a nice smile but maybe it would help. Though you're dead serious, share yourself.

You worked, you completed, you cried, now prepare for visitation.

THESE QUIPS ARE BRUTAL REVERSALS

These quips are brutal reversals of reality marking discovery according to Koestler in the sixties.

Don't turn against him just cuz everyone hates him. It happens to genius, saints, all great men.

The genius of the picturestrips is pattern recognition--the thing lost with alcohol in the system.

Drinking brings anosognosia--loss of pattern recognition--as life fails from the mal-adaptation.

Anosognasia or inability to see your patterns means you're sunk as life takes a downturn.

To win at life I have to adapt every moment as situations change--not a "gameplan", how deranged.

If I don't adapt by nipping it in the bud I'll go down a rabbit hole and some last decades--NO!

It doesn't have to have a meaning, it's purpose is to evoke thought in you.

The work ethic is about making good use of your TIME not just slaving for chump change.

EPILOGUE

Once you see the light on the creep let your friends corner, isolate and shove him out quick.

WORK HARD FOR COMPLETION

It's not a matter of working hard for completion, but clearing the head so it's automatically done.

Turn it all off, put music on, clear the head and now everything will be done/nothing left undone.

Anyone great is criticized--always, remember that. But women are worse, whether thin or fat.

Due to the resistances to genius, the less is happening the more is gonna happen to please us.

My greatest lesson of my lifetime: Stop asking why they keep doing it and stop allowing it.

I don't sell myself, if you like me or don't it's not my business I just proceed in creative health.

What if it's a child tied up out in the elements without escape? How would YOU like it, creep?

You're gonna be hearing from people, this is incredible.

It's what I do. It's not even a lost art, it's an invented one and what fun!

An invention finally realized on earth after fifty years of work.

First I find the pictures then I assemble them then I add the words and it only took forty years.

I don't sell myself I just do my work.

Why am I dedicated to the picturestrip theory? Cuz I see how it fits together in pure synchronicity.

EPILOGUE

If it's a sin it'll block your destiny so no matter how trivial it seems, watch where you've been.

Just read classic novels or the bible and old movies are a marvel.

You get into those cards and in time you'll start to fail and your Godly predestiny of no avail.

God has plans to prosper you but not with those cards which is the devil and familiar spirits too.

New cosmology for y'all, a theoretical Taj Mahal.

START GROUPS ON TIME

Should start the bible study on time not wait for stragglers to walk in--never adapt to them!

Wasting time chatting/eating and when the last straggler walks in they finally start the meeting.

There's four personalities in the house besides us: dogs and cats.

In a fallen world dogs must be fenced.

Be this way, I behoove: In the old west when you saw smoke from neighbors it was time to move.

We put up with stuff in the past and it's hardly a blast. Now our map is nip it in the bud, at last.

I took you in and you abused me in turn.

Stop being a victim because you've always known he'll do it again/and again.

He calls it a small thing but it is no small thing in fact it's everything so wake up, play, sing.

I'm shaking, heart is racing, feel like retching. God help me it's so dark here, so cold/wretched.

EPILOGUE

What is worse--the trauma of losing him or enduring what you found on his PC again/and again?

That last little mistake led to a massive breach of trust.

What would your mother say if she knew what you found out about him?

You don't want someone who's disgusting cuz you don't wanna yell at him.

God didn't choose the demons bothering you so stop lumping all together like birds of a feather.

PLANT SEED, WAIT FOR HARVEST

I've planted the seed and am waiting for the harvest which doesn't happen overnight but it must.

Whether I am gracious to everyone or finicky with how I give out my gifts, their demands bring rifts.

My cute puppy wants a hug to make sure mommy still loves him before he creates more bedlam.

it's a two-speed week: activity/work vs. rest and relaxation. However I always end up the same.

It takes someone facing death with nothing to lose to finally tell you the truth and these are few.

Ultimately woman finds success in her own home because that's where she belongs.

Let em go and never think of them. These people are cruel as their sin.

Many daughters have done virtuously, nobly and well, but you excel them all. Proverbs 31: 29

"Where did she ever get that much money to do that" she cackled, caddy as ever as she wrinkled.

EPILOGUE

It's ok to be glamorous and have a ball. Sparkle it up in good clean fun before it's all over for y'all.

I just can't go there, I prefer not to go there so kindly stop talking about it: shut up I do declare.

ACTING OUT FILTHY NARRATIVES

It will take you decades to get over this opprobrium you've brought to yourself and fam, ma'am.

The map is not the territory. Stop saying you're doing something when you're not, really.

Time passes, generations die out, everything's new but that doesn't mean good and I feel blue.

Music is mathematics unless it's by an ass.

Can you imagine how freaked out your pets are with all the chaos you create (and all electronic)?

You must be free to express it, or silence.

Be above all questions. Unless you're in sin, on the begging end.

Holes in the sequencing indicate not enough units in the strip.

That's not it, sister. The way you act is NOT IT.

Build it, be it, they will come.

Holes in the sequencing indicate less units in the strip so stop saying it's too much/miss the point.

The intelligence required in picturestripping is pure Pattern Recognition, the basis of the IQ test.

Between Harriet Craig and (the old) Rosanne I'll choose the puritan stickler-for-order harridan.

EPILOGUE

It's the next project, that's all--no deadlines or other anti-genius forces, we're done with this.

It's not that we're Goody two-shoes but that we make a lot of any and all events during our day.

Very busy vacationing after a long project and keeping work out.

Tho' feelings are liars, they're still strong.

EARLY BAD RELATIONSHIPS

You always were so puerile, silly, shallow, superficial, social, petty, gossipy but I loved you truly.

An unhappy person is contagious. Mike Murdock

All afternoon you gotta party to get ready/prepare for tomorrow's creative work being artsy.

Extend his life by leaving him alone.

Strange behavior unexplained: It's all demons or being weak, untamed.

What they see as arrogance ("it's not from me but from God") is really the greatest humility.

Brain power: the main problem is being tracked rather than allowing your own genius to blast.

On Sunday you should sit and think, look out the window, you're the best and they're rinky dink.

If confused or fatigued get off the keys and let the mind wonder, please.
You've done enough today, always get away.

It'll all get done--completion is fun. Your only problem is worrying it won't/feeling under the gun.

All you need is the beginning and then it'll all carry through and completion is part of it too.

EPILOGUE

Never force the fit, it's more important to get away and stop work for the day.

Spend your energy/time not working so the subconscious can take over in fullest completion.

Everything is opposite: To work, stop work. To lose weight, eat everything in site then stop, alright?

The way I like it is the way it is. Get on up, stay on the scene. James Brown

A lot of dead heroes got nervous.

FAKE INTELLECTS

Never zeroing in, talking around the subject--hoping they'll hit something, intellectually abject.

You have a powerful and healthy vision so don't be surprised if not one thing happens before then.

Your vision is so high it's missed altogether until that moment when it all comes together.

You'll need a team, right on your beam, seeing what you see: a new scene and how serene!

You're so futuristic they can't take it cuz it's disparate from their corny take on it, dumbed down twits.

Think back to your fishing, camping, hiking; when God and nature was the only good/right thing.

Stop work, switching from active to receptivity. The work'll get done but you'll also have plenty.

Urgent work, forcing the fit, worthless accomplishments: let mind wonder instead/focus on moment.

Watch movies from your childhood era to take you back before trauma of losing your America.

EPILOGUE

If you're forcing the fit/going along for fame, you'll come crashing down esp. public reputation.

If afraid of offending you'll lose all creativity, believe me. Gotta be free to create & offend me.

Having learned of strife she became a complete shut-in later in life.

Superior man watches for miracles like a cat watches a mouse hole as he comes together whole.

Hardly anyone has opportunity to go deep inside. So much chaotic social blocks the high prize.

THE SAINTS REJECT EXPECTATIONS

Expectations, invites and yokes: the saints leave off one after another until life is a happy joke.

One obligation after another, the saint disentrenches from all networks, personal appetites, quirks.

Repent of and seek freedom from all the things you unwisely think you should be doing, too.

Once having embarked on your inner journey the social world loses charm, you're bored/alarmed.

By using a computer you can either get smarter every minute or dumbed down in the gutter, finished.

Falling outa structure is like slipping into cozy pajamas.

Stop remorsing over things when the devil had control. You were trapped being weak and sold.

Why not assume all will go right rather than wrong? The latter's from the past/liberal throng.

Gotta have a team, there's just too much creativity.

EPILOGUE

Do your work, assume for the best, cast your care and rest in God.

You went thru hell but that was just overcoming (training)--now retirement will be great/swell.

How amazing: just one slight change and your whole life transforms as it rearranges/is normal.

My work is my life so if you're helping me, what does it say?

Collaboration may seem a key to success but more than likely it just degrades/creates a mess.

How to get a man: love him, put him first for a change.

A prophet is not a man who tells the future; he is a man who tells the truth. Harold Kushner

What can I say, I've tucked it away and don't wanna discuss it today.

DON'T LET MIND BE TRACKED

Don't let the mind be tracked even with great movies. Keep stepping back into nothing/happiness.

Just when things look invincible, impossible--it can still be done cuz fighting giants is FUN.

Work is my fun, my fun is my work. When it all fits together it's a thrill or a perk.

Obama was the greatest gift to the conservative movement we've ever seen. Thank you, fiend!

Best cure for delusions about democracy is a five minute conversation with an average voter. Churchill

What's it all for? If it's just for image (magic) it will always fail, you'll be a public fool and floored.

EPILOGUE

This whole way of thinking has taken hold, they can't think beyond this and they're very bold.

That's your generation so you reflect it but the rest of us know it's a bunch of bull and reject it.

The new religion/totalitarian ideology is political correctness though what it's based on is totally false.

As it's not based on reality, the new cosmology must be learned by rote--make a mistake, you're out.

WE SWIM IN MUDDY WATERS

By linking up with a phony feminist group filled with filthy language she became disgusting too.

They push the button marked "racist" then get whatever they want fastest.

American exceptionalism: designed by geniuses to minimize government.

And you silly KKK (krazy kollege kids) are pawns, tools of global dons.

Gun-grabbers beware: Schools are already gun-free zones, that's why mass shooters go there.

She's a very nice lady but not a Calvinist and let's em get away with way too much (out to lunch).

Gun ownership does not correlate with the homicide rate, rather there's an inverse relationship.

Gun control is not crime control, in fact crime quickly skyrockets in gun free zones, ya know.

The edgy artist gets attention in a debauched generation but how far do you go with this perversion?

I really think you should know what you're talking about before putting this crap out there, beware.

EPILOGUE

They're the sum total of everything: it's all about narcissism, all about "me" even for salvation they're key.

Definition of mad scientist: wants to find eternal life without Jesus Christ.

One of the biggest punishments is fascination with the occult which ends in hellishness and rot.

When conscience is seared your natural revulsion to nastiness is dead and things get worse instead.

GOOD LUCK CROSSING THE LINE

Good luck if you're crossed that line. You're now a nasty swine but can't see it tho' others divide.

A nasty woman is a terrible, hideous thing but they actually think it's good, sophisticated, worthy.

A wife of noble character is her husband's crown but a disgraceful wife is decay in his bones. Prov 12: 4

Pockets of crime are in blue areas of gun bans.

If everyone has guns as in Switzerland crime goes way down cuz everyone's wonderin'.

Take our guns, make us into sitting ducks. Criminals can always get guns so gun control sux.

They wanna take away the great equalizer enabling old ladies or kids to fight against gangsters.

True art doesn't need your soft porn to push it along, it's cheap and weak not smart and strong.

You don't realize it cuz it's mundane to you but you're making an ass of yourself by conforming to.

When insanity becomes mundane reality you just fall into the popular groove thinking nothing of it too.

EPILOGUE

The only thing that is charming and intelligent is the True Self not you conforming to them/that ass.

I hear you/see you mimicking those debauched broads and losing all class cuz you think it's mod.

If you have to mimic someone let it be your grandma not those debauched broads looking so odd.

There were times in history of collective insanity/the contagion of madness and now we see this.

ANOSOGNOSIA: BLIND TO YOUR CONDITION

You don't realize how far you've fallen into decay and shame due to the influence of those dames.

They aren't even pretty or slim, they're fat little piglets cuz that's the love-me-anyway feminists.

Soros: 1000 busses to bring in 2nd amendment protestors and it's all fake but I think you know this.

They know nothing, is just contagious lunacy. But we're ruled by kids and it's dangerous tyranny.

Armed citizens aren't the cause--gangbangers, lunatics and terrorists don't abide our gun laws.

The social herd is like cackling thorns on a fire, it grits my nerves until I call for One who's higher.

The very idea that I'd have to survey the lay of the land before speaking in order to not offend?

I gotta speak from the cuff, not think about what's too much or enough--spontaneous not phony stuff.

If I had to always think how you're gonna take it before I say something it's like being muted/crazy.

EPILOGUE

Now that you know the kids are crazy you don't have to adapt to them in any way and better not I say.

All men are sinners but please, not this crap. Gambling, anything but please don't tell me that.

Why don't people answer? Cuz there's so much going on and it's better for you and them, hiding.

"We all have sins and to have a gambling husband would be bad but this is worse", she said.

Jesus sacrificed, Allah conquered with vice--who shows mercy/loves you tho' you sin > twice?

Hey that's dirty man. You guys are sick!

Think of it: an entire generation: debauched! Not just them, their grandmothers too, gone.

The way they act is embarrassing.

Millennials are marching madness.

Let's not dress this up--you're going for a walk with a banner. Katie Hopkins

FEMALES FACILITATE SOCIETAL COLLAPSE

To facilitate the decay of society you absolutely must get women's minds first so kids are cursed.

Don't be dumb, she's not gonna let it go. It's in her craw and she'll milk it till the cows come home.

I'd hate to get into a fight with the amazingly articulate woman you married, like a steel claw: scary.

Disney's magical world for children was nothing but brainwash from the pit of hell to create villains.

EPILOGUE

Liberal twists: If I say it doesn't exist that means it exists, especially spoken of supposed racists.

Jesus Christ brings a revival or a dogfight. His own family thought he was crazy. Charles Lawson

TRUE CHRISTIANITY IS "UNACCEPTABLE"

True Christianity is "unacceptable" so we don't wanna present ourselves badly to the rabble.

Psychology, philosophy, education does NOT make man free. It's only the bible which makes you SEE.

Religion is judged by it's fruits. Ask any Muslim woman or see Hinduism--check out India too.

I believe three in one, one in three and the One in the middle died for me.

Sinner has no remorse over who he murdered, just himself "not treated right by God, targeted".

God takes pity on those who fear him so be God-fearing and live.

It's just unbelievable how you believe in princess many-words but that is just how it works.

Repent of your sins then a humble and contrite spirit (cuz you fear it) draws men to Christ, know it.

As he hung himself/his guts fell out on the floor we witnessed the ignominious end of a traitor, to pray for.

Turn off the self-love garbage, get rid of the self-love preachers, and get right with God.

I don't trust many words cuz the truth can be said simply: their ship is sinking thus the shooting.

Pastors locked up for hate speech: gov-unapproved.

EPILOGUE

Arrogance and ignorance are bedfellows.

It's so horrible turn off the news. They would do something like that from desperation blues.

Some people are better off hand to mouth rather than a big bank account.

NEVER GIVE INTO PRONOUNS/NEW JARGON

When you meet fake feminists like Trudeau, insist on "mankind" not the correction "peoplekind".

With those numbers they could run this country any time but they're too shiftless and lazy, slime.

See it, end it: nip it in the bud like a Trumpist.

Le Bron James should shut up and dribble cuz he knows nothing and comes off as dumb/simple.

No compromise with those the essence of betrayal—the ache of emotions severed and denial.

Necromancy is occult and it's not ol' dad you're talking to it's a demon who's gonna get your goat.

Evil spirits of idolatry include ancestral worship—go, get out of the people now then LOOK UP.

Necromancy—talking to the dead—is as evil as divination and witchcraft so Christians, stop that.

Pray for cultural reversal from all this programming from Disney which includes pornography.

Trump represents a divine delay in judgment and a reprieve—why not help him to succeed?

Are you hot and passionate for Jesus or lukewarm and putting on a show?

EPILOGUE

A male feminist keeping "peace at any price" in a home filled with females so compromised?

Your binge-watching (one soft-porn movie after another) is just as non-Christian, my brother.

Can't people just watch movies with beautiful scenery and great scripts--not sexualized by twits?

Soft porn is just as bad (obscene language, big visible boobs): accepted but more suggestive.

GRATUITOUS SEX IS PANDEMIC

Gratuitous sex (out of the blue) is pandemic in European or Hollywood movies since the 70's.

Italian movie was one hour of beautiful scenery and villas--then gratuitous sex making us bilious.

Soft porn is the wider category and accepted yet the most insidious in the hearts of the elected.

Appreciation of scenery, villas and scripts--the finer things of life--not this hex or attempted fix.

Men should marry not burn in this crap and see how it wrecks their life and mind changing mental maps

Husbands who are into porn will be yelling at their wives every time and in fact it's a sure sign.

We don't wanna see that, ok? Some sinner's vision of the sex act--a terrible thing common today.

You dirty my life and mind with movies you make, fakes. Armed guards/my guns you wanna take.

Tarot, astrology--there's some truth in all things but God's above it all totally/occult is ungodly.

EPILOGUE

A couple are watching TV, age seventy. Suddenly we see a big-boobed bare-chested slut, you see.

Soft porn is my new target just hope he won't suicide over it.

The anti-establishment become the pro-establishment having enjoyed the trappings of office.

When we saw massive liberal bureaucracies fail those in the know got outa the California hell.

CONTRIBUTE TO YOUR HOUSEHOLD

If you're watching movies all day you're a dry well to the household, all contributions gone.

What are you contributing, you bore? Sucked into a vortex of media but nothing coming out anymore.

No man would ever sit thru a woman's meeting: so boring in fact, an hour I'll never get back.

You waste your own time so wanna waste mine.

They say they're "fashionably late" when it's just their ego that loves to make em all wait.

Don't call it "hanging with God's people" when it's just chattering like all the silly sheeple.

The virtue signaling going on in women's gatherings is very boring but it's all about identity.

In women's meetings there's usually one doing the talking while the others are listening intently.

These aren't days of Roy Rogers. We got creeps coming to Cane Beds just like all neighborhoods.

How interesting: the far right is actually the new centrism marking a return to historical realism.

EPILOGUE

As Trudeau's progressivism is dying and depleting Canadian conservatism is exploding and Christian.

SECULAR LIBERALISM

Secular liberalism has no room for white men having painted itself to the corner of identity politics.

Trump: Call the cops and tip the neighbor's crazy so they go get the guns and maybe arrest him?

Do we adapt to the left's superstitious hysteria or revert to reason and logic in our America?

They've invested so much into this they can't deal with the terrible unforeseen consequences.

You're gonna punish me cuz a lunatic shot up schools? So with home invasion, I can't shoot?

It's so disgusting. Men having fun with their butt buddies telling their wives they've gone fishing.

He always says it's a small thing but it's no small thing it hurts her so deeply she's sick and trembling.

The lady said "I'm very scared of it happening again--another way of saying I just don't trust him."

Survivor's clue: It will never be over and you don't know the half of it.

We all know that people can't get well for other people if they don't even see themselves as sick/evil.

What's to stop him from doing it again? His love for you? That didn't work five times re: sin.

Lesson: It's not that he did it it's that he would do it, he's into it.

The lady said "he hurt me so much I can't breathe and naturally he minimizes it." I hear this.

EPILOGUE

Women vote like their husbands cuz that's why they married (affinity) not cuz he's making them.

What about husbands voting as their wives say, Hillary? That's more likely to be the case, silly.

Why are big corporations allowing radical leftists into company decisions regarding language?

CONTEST OF STUPIDITY

The politically correct march is like a contest of stupidity as our jaw drops with each new absurdity.

Interlocking jealousy triangles: if I pet those dogs my own dogs might react with fear and anger.

Christian men must learn the importance of not hurting their wives by what they see with their eyes.

Obama shipped guns into Mexico to blame the second amendment and kill those who object.

Taking all our identities: Trudeau the worst globalist banned the word "mother" just today.

Banning "mother" and "father" is not tolerance but taking our identities and a cultural slaughter.

Banning word "mother" (may make someone feel bad) is not tolerance but an identity-crusher.

If you want smaller government, white males and white married females is your demographic.

You cross that line (of debauchery of swine) then you're on the treadmill to hell without shame/guilt.

I wouldn't go down that path lest you be cast in that light as a shrew. It's sickening, blue, dirty too.

EPILOGUE

Your generation's nuts so stop reflecting the ASS and think for your own self so later no remorse.

Experiments on dogs and monkeys--the SJW's don't care about that, they just scream as always.

Do anything you want, you're never get our guns cuz that leaves us defenseless against thugs.

By saying "men" I mean "peoplekind"--everyone--a nonpersonal pronoun and most traditional.

So you have the money to make a complete fool of yourself, in public no less.

They create false narratives--to protect you from--but you don't know it as they dumb you down.

Can't do your destiny if always thinking about the past. You're not getting any younger/have a blast.

DAILY FASTARIAN: ONE WAY OUT

Eat whatever you want, it's only one digestive burn a day and it all goes through by mass evacuation.

When I eat it's the most calorically dense, a cowboy thinks of that. Levoy Finnicum

I don't look at em as "meals" but just ONE "digestive burn" and "exposure" then not one morsel.

Fruits and vegetables are the only real ant-acids since everything else causes it.

The densest nutrition is in the greens so if you can't eat kale, get romaine and eat it every day.

Tho' you may eat chips the greens are a buffer and delete effects.

Never take diet advice from a pagan. If they're into tarot cards take your own advice/drop em.

EPILOGUE

Americans were very hard-working people. Not stay home around a juicer they had to eat and run.

I've never desired rabbit food. Just fill the tank, stop the pangs then get back to work, soothed.

They carbed up in the morning then worked all day. They had delicious fats with it too so don't tell me.

If you make it he may not eat it so just fill his fridge with the best ingredients.

EAT FAT TO LOSE WEIGHT

If you can't lose weight you need more fats like butter--high fat diet will change your life altogether.

She mixes fats with starches, breaking all rules. That's cuz it's only one digestive burn she argues.

No digestive fire, there it sits, body reads it as an allergen or pathogen and you've had it man.

Not living on rabbit food hungry all the time needing so much but starch with fat then no lunch.

A substantial breakfast is how mom said to eat so that's how it's gonna be and I'm so hunger-free.

Fat/starch delays digestion to the lower colon so all day long you're not groanin' and can work glowin'.

Mom was mad when I ate lettuce for breakfast not starting out on my best foot calorically dense.

It's the American way: a big breakfast then work all day. Fruit or salad for breakfast? NO WAY.

The very idea that us hardworking Americans have to hang around a frig/juicer to get our nutrients.

Fuel the tank, fast all day.

EPILOGUE

Can't create with three meals in the gut.

How to lose weight: skip dinner, don't eat lunch. Just do breakfast, a bunch.

Bakery is fine unless it's false then you build a big body like a horse.

GET HEALTHY CANDY

Candy addicts: Get it outa your system then reject totally cuz it's all fillers not like the old days.

In all things it is canola oil, soy, fructose corn syrup, gum but in different proportions/flavorings.

Scottish Shortbread (butter/sugar/flour) is better than all those chemicals and oils, the main killers.

Fat acceptance is hooked to thin privilege as we cascade down to this cultural mental illness.

GMO causes massive cancer, deformities and gene drift but globalist monsters say "it's the best."

GMO side effects are just old tech, now new stuff's rolling out and we'll be even more bloated up.

Everything is the same ingredients in different proportions and flavorings and all illegal in Europe.

This isn't candy, it's chemicals. Candy is real: chocolate, nuts, honey, sugar, butter, flavor natural.

Aborted fetal tissue (AFT) to flavorings is based on murder therefore it's a ritual sacrifice/avoid em.

Most oils created by God have an armory of defense against this and that, anti-everything that's bad.

Avocado oil much better than coconut oil—the one they see as gold.

EPILOGUE

Scotch ate shortbread or it stores well instead: 1/3 sugar, 1/3 flour, 1/3 butter and pinch salt.

Way to life: skip dinner and don't do lunch.

Read ingredients--it ALL has the same poison just in different proportions. Soy, corn syrup, chemicals.

It's ok to eat candy if it's real ingredients, a quick way to get nutrients and sugar (energy) deliverance.

FAST FISH: GET INGREDIENTS

Fast fish is composed of the same ingredients as bakery--poison, but Europeans get the real thing.

Don't tell em what to eat just point out the cheat and they find their own way back to the real treats.

50% of our food is banned in Europe--think of that. Americans are so unsensuous eating crap.

Grandma's cookies and candies were such energizers and always digested just right, outa sight.

Don't tell em what to eat cuz then you're a darn clique again, a liberal social club and dietary tyranny.

Man is like dogs, omnivorous. We can adapt to many diets so don't tell em what to eat just be selective.

Oatmeal, bread, butter, dairy, eggs and bacon: Just a normal breakfast for centuries with Americans.

Her grandad was a centenarion living on buttered popcorn and beer--re: diet, we just can't say for sure.

Her grandad was a centenarion living on buttered popcorn and beer--re: diet, we just can't say for sure.

We love shortbread cuz it makes us eat it otherwise we're not interested.

EPILOGUE

Eat, then that's it--it's all behind you. Now it's fasting consciousness, enjoy the luscious view!

I LOVE SHORTBREAD FASTING

Shortbread's used for Scottish armies or efficient fastarian satieties and is a cultural treasury.

Don't have to weigh, it's how my clothes fit: time to fast and feel legit.

Provide structure by a family breakfast, at least.

Popcorn is a delivery system for the butter.

Eat, don't eat, trip.

I have discovered the trick of fat with starch which delays digestion (satiety) for joyous fastin'.

Fats with starches allows eating less for satiety, delays digestion not hungry and flat gut, skinny.

I can take one digestive burn a day. Any more (to eat again) and it's all-night hell to pay.

Lotsa butter collapses calories (less eating) so you can happily go all day without food, flying.

Boil water, add Ramen otherwise tangerines are good for em.

One quarter of what you eat keeps you alive, the rest keeps your doctor alive. Egyptian proverb

Two grilled cheese sandwiches, fast a day. It's gotta be calorically dense to live this way.

It's hard to fast 24 hours daily on one meal of fruit or salad. You gotta have more, then you'll love it.

Don't ever take diet advice from a pagan and soft porn is just as bad, though forgiven.

EPILOGUE

Go right for the superfood, like red bell pepper--it'll open up your throat and voice too.

Never ask a pagan witch filled with vice for diet advice.

Weight loss program: in the mornin' have bread/butter with jam then buttered popcorn now fastin'.

EAT FAT BUT ALWAYS FAST

My parents ate butter--every meal and day--and stayed skinny that way.

How to love yourself and life better: Smother everything in butter.

Nothing is more delicious than butter and have you deprived yourself (of best food) believing nutters?

Not oils like canola, soy and all that lethal crap. But butter, the thing most loved by mom and dad.

When did cancer become epidemic? When we exchanged butter for lethal chemistry.

Parisian king opened his windows to take a deep breath of the morning air and got sewage/beware.

The chemically sensitive stop leaving home completely-- doing anything to avoid being sickly.

You resurface and they say "are you well now" cuz they don't know about total load--a sliding variable.

By me not fixing food (slacking off) he becomes over reliant on candy for satiety/not good missy.

Walmart bakery is deliciously made from flavorings, soy, corn syrup and other poisons we gulp.

How could anything so delicious as Walmart Bakery be 100% made from chemicals? But it is, truly.

EPILOGUE

Read the bakery label--it should say fruit, flour, sugar and butter (different combos)--not chemicals!

It's simply shocking to eat a delicious cookie then belch with bubbles and acid all night and day.

Dive into the pies and cakes first then end the day with the best not the worst now fast/end curse.

MEN WERE HANDSOME, WOMEN PRETTY

The men were so handsome and the women so pretty and it's not just the food it's all toxicity.

Everyone looked so good in the fifties before there was fructose corn syrup on all things.

Start with acid end with alkaline that's the only way assured you won't have acid reflux at night.

Acid then alkaline, just skip dinner every time.

I solved the problem, no more acid at night. Acid am, alkaline noon, skip dinner, sleep tight.

Lifelong heartburn, gone. As me how.

Acid morning alkaline noon just skip dinner see me swoon.

Acid foods: breakfast goodies like pancakes, french toast, omelets, lotsa butter/starch/sweet.

Alkaline foods: fruits/veggies/roots. Stick to that for noon now just skip dinner: thin as flute.

The more nothing is happening the more it's going to soon so store up strength/rest in your room.

With discoveries in all fields it's unremunerated work for decades and then that one big check.

THE KK PICTURESTRIP
THE SUPERIOR INSTRUMENT
INVENTOR: KAREN KELLOCK PH.D.

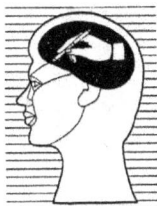

This is a new theory in psychology. Please see www.karenkellock.org for the picturestrip version of Manual for Superior Men.   According to Koestler, all landmark theories are presented in picture-strip format (right-left integration) to bring on the "aha" experience of the formula (the characteristic of all new paradigms).   The picturestrip instrument has been proven by neurophysiologists to be the superior tool for insight (Pribram, Stanford). Chromo-Symmetric-Kinostatic Motion: As the pictures connect (by color, composition and texture) to resemble each other, the subject matter goes bananas—varies widely—and the discrepancy brings = INSIGHT.   Movies (inferior) = every frame the same. Picturestrips (superior) = every frame radically different though connected visually creating the necessary discrepancy and acting as a hypnotic pushing through cognitive dissonance to acceptance of the NEW THEORY.

TO STUDENTS OF THEORY AND INSTRUMENT:

The instrument: same in color but shifts in subject, creating discrepancy and then insight as the viewer is forced out of his frame of reference. God put this universe together and it's about vibration and that's color. More they resemble each other the more the discrepancy with radically different subject matter. It really gets exciting when it all starts to fit together then with a head full of steam destiny takes over. Picturestrips are not like a jigsaw puzzle where it snaps into place and you got that piece, please. Picturestrip talent is a three-part process: selection, sequentialization and the words. Sequentialization is the talent or intelligence of seeing what's missing or what doesn't belong. Everything fits, it all fits. All is synchronicity on earth and that makes the

EPILOGUE

picturestrip legit. Color is wave frequency and vibration and through the Law of Affinitization it all fits and what a trip! See how it all fits--color and composition--and with words how it catapults you to understanding. A word fitly spoken and in due season is like apples of gold in settings of silver. Prov 25: 11 Picturestrips are called "mind-shattering thought art". Just to appreciate art you're in the right brain. Most don't see it, clouded by sensual drives and sin. *The test of a discovery is: does it work?*

KK Message to Students

Why do the best talents ripen late? Since they bring the most people to God they are the most great. Say it in such a beautiful way they can't dispute it. Beauty saves the day and does the work. Slow it down towards the end, allowing insights to come in. You can't have personality without the knowledge to pull it off so just shut up. You must be able to express rage without profanity and that takes eternity, regarded as a rarity. *Speak against* for just as supreme court decisions mimic popular opinion, so too science says the popular is ok with em.

There happens to be this cult where if you're not in you're out: snobs. It even happens to patriots: ingroups, outgroups. They do whatever they want, promptly forget it but meanwhile their soul gets ugly, decrepit and they can't fixit. They take every opportunity to zing you from jealousy so just stay home and avert the tragedy. We must escape the mind-numbing orthodoxy of racial diversity (Jarad Taylor). No matter how deep you get God always has an escape plan ready--just get clear then stay steady.

Race is an expression of the same thing as love of family. Race is aligned with natural law of man, not like these social constructs--a house built on sand. Deniers of race are at war with truth. We deal with facts not fools. We will be a bio-mass, a Tijuana with everyone degraded to that level. No matter what you want to believe you can't defy natural law like gravity. Believing in reality--race--raises the inwardly dead to new life. You can suppress the natural law but never defeat it. You can drive nature out the front door but it'll come through the back door. Thomas Jefferson Reality is truth which shines in the dark and can never be put out. Truth will come back, so let out a shout!

EPILOGUE

The saints are **BOLD**. Must have panache: flamboyance, confidence, self-assurance, style, flair, dash, verve, zest and your uniquely vital energy. Steady: I know things are SO fast but you go slow--make each moment perfect then collect them all. Without knowledge pulling it off you'll slip into trendy pat crap and be mocked. See them as a liberal disgrace, virtue signaling then falling flat on their face. I say, why give em a chance to hurt me? There's always jealousies so stay home and avoid the silly. Come out of your focus (tunnel vision) and become receptive (enjoy living and accomplishment).

Spouse helped me not by funding but protecting me while I worked, being a fence as it were. You people are too into phones: entry points of demons. Thank You God for completion.

**If we're gonna be a minority in our own country,
what was it all for?**

**"Union Jack not a symbol of pride but oppression"
--UK going thru the same trashing as America.**

**Fearing people is a dangerous trap but trusting
the Lord means safety. Proverbs 29: 25**

**Manage the herd around you or give up your goals.
Cuz they'll waste your time and your soul.**

**Europe's dead. Refinement, the Renaissance,
man's highest potential, science, God, history, charm.**

It's Jesus plus nothing.

AUTHOR BIO

Karen Kellock Ph.D.

Ph.D Political Psychology, UCI 1976
Post-Doctoral: UCI Medical School
Department of Psychiatry
Grants NIMH, NIAAA

Ph.D. dissertation "A Systems-Theoretic View of Pathologic Interaction" made an early mark as the "Wife of the Alcoholic Syndrome". Postdoctoral research at UCI Medical, Dept. of Psychiatry on the systems surrounding pathology on NIMH and NIAAA federal grants: The Contagion of Madness: The Psychology of Neurotic Interaction and Pathological Systems. Therapy tool Therapeutic Playwriting introduced the play Mary and Murv: Gruesome Twosomes in the Alcoholic Marriage. She taught Abnormal Psychology and Pathological Systems Theory at UC and CSU campuses and developed "the Debris Theory of Disease" in 100 books and website: (www.karenkellock.org).

www.ingramcontent.com/pod-product-compliance
Lightning Source LLC
Chambersburg PA
CBHW072113270326
41931CB00010B/1547